2 Esdras

To Howard,

With my compliments,

Bruce.

GW00776538

2 ESDRAS

Bruce W. Longenecker

Sheffield Academic Press

For David and Tamara Chaffee, David and Ellen Kupp,
and Sean and Sally Robertshaw
friends who help to make this age feel a little bit more like the next!

Copyright © 1995 Sheffield Academic Press

Published by Sheffield Academic Press Ltd
Mansion House
19 Kingfield Road
Sheffield, S11 9AS
England

Printed on acid-free paper in Great Britain
by The Cromwell Press
Melksham, Wiltshire

British Library Cataloguing in Publication Data

A catalogue record for this book is available
from the British Library

ISBN 1-85075-726-7

Contents

Contents

Preface

A guide to 2 Esdras is, by definition, a peculiar thing, since 2 Esdras itself consists of three independently written documents: 4 Ezra (2 Esdras 3–14), 5 Ezra (2 Esdras 1–2) and 6 Ezra (2 Esdras 15–16). The first of these is the intriguing Jewish apocalypse of the late first century ce, while the latter two are later Christian texts that have come to be attached to 4 Ezra. The first eight chapters of this guide deal with the Jewish apocalypse, while the ninth chapter examines the two shorter Christian texts.

The writing of this guide has had significant consequences for me, following on from my reacquaintance with the text of 4 Ezra after a few years' hiatus. If the theme of transformation is important to a proper understanding of 4 Ezra, it also marks out the development of my own views on 4 Ezra. A previous exploration of 4 Ezra resulted in the publication of my *Eschatology and the Covenant: A Comparison of 4 Ezra and Romans 1-11* (JSNTSup 57; Sheffield: JSOT Press, 1991). While I stand by a great deal that appeared in that project (especially in relation to the first half of 4 Ezra), my views have changed on a few significant points. The result is that this guide offers a much different (and less controversial) reading of the second half of 4 Ezra than that earlier work.

I owe a debt of thanks to the following: to Professor Michael Knibb, for his guidance of this project; to St John's College (Durham, England), and in particular to David Day and John Pritchard, for providing me with a study term in which the writing of this guide was a primary project; and to Fiona Bond, now my wife, for being understanding when the writing of this guide encroached upon our all-too-infrequent times together.

Bruce W. Longenecker
Cambridge
January 1995

Primary Sources, Translations and Commentaries

Primary Sources and Translations:

R.L. Bensly, *The Fourth Book of Ezra*, with an Introduction by M.R. James (Texts and Studies 3.2; Cambridge: Cambridge University Press, 1895). An edited version of the Latin manuscripts.

R.J. Bidawid, '4 Esdras', in *The Old Testament in Syriac According to the Peshitta Version* (part 4, facs. 3; Leiden: Brill, 1973). A reproduction of the seventh-century Syriac version.

G.H. Box, *The Apocalypse of Ezra* (London: SPCK, 1917). An English translation of the Syriac manuscript of 4 Ezra.

A.F.J. Klijn, *Der lateinische Text der Apokalypse des Esra* (Texte und Untersuchungen 131; Berlin: Akademie Verlag, 1983). An edited version of the Latin manuscripts.

A.F.J. Klijn, *Die Esra-Apokalypse (IV. Esra)* (Die Griechischen Christlichen Schriftsteller der ersten Jahrhunderte; Berlin: Akademie Verlag, 1992). A German translation of 4 Ezra, prefaced by a detailed methodological explanation and including extensive textual notes.

B.M. Metzger, 'The Fourth Book of Ezra', in *Old Testament Pseudepigrapha* (vol. 1, ed. J.H. Charlesworth; London: Darton, Longman & Todd, 1983), pp. 514-559. A brief introduction to 4 Ezra is followed by an English translation of 2 Esdras 1-16 from Bensley's Latin text, with minor textual notes. This translation of 2 Esdras also appears (with slight variation) in The Revised Standard Version and the New Revised Standard Version of the Apocrypha.

J. Schreiner, *Das 4. Buch Esra* (ed. W.G. Kümmel et al.; Jüdische Schriften aus hellenistisch-römischer Zeit; Gütersloh: Mohn, 1981). A German translation, with an introduction and brief textual notes.

M.E. Stone, *The Armenian Version of IV Ezra* (University of Pennsylvania Armenian Texts and Studies 1; Missoùla: Scholars Press, 1979). An edited version of the twenty-two Armenian manuscripts, with a translation.

B. Violet, *Die Esra-Apokalypse (IV. Esra). Erster Teil: Die Überlieferung* (Die griechischen christlichen Schriftsteller 18; Leipzig: Hinrichs Verlag, 1910). Six columns juxtapose an edited Latin text with the Syriac, Ethiopic and two Arabic texts (translated into German), and an Armenian text (translated into Latin).

Commentaries:

G.H. Box, *The Ezra-Apocalypse* (London: Pitman, 1912); also appeared as '4 Ezra', in *The Apocrypha and Pseudepigrapha of the Old Testament* (vol. 2, ed. R.H. Charles; Oxford: Clarendon Press, 1913), pp. 542-624. The standard commentary in English for years, and with many helpful insights, if somewhat outdated in methodology.

L. Gry, *Les dites prophétiques d'Esdras (IV Esdras)* (2 vols.; Paris: Geuthner, 1930). A somewhat unbalanced commentary; extensive and detailed, but postulating unusual reconstructions of the text.

H. Gunkel, 'Das vierte Buch Esra', in *Die Apokryphen und Pseudepigraphen des alten Testaments* (vol. 2, ed. E. Kautzsch; Tübingen: Mohr, 1900), pp. 331-402. A German standard that still continues to exert significant influence, especially in highlighting the psychological dynamics of 4 Ezra with regard to the author's own inner turmoil.

M.A. Knibb, 'Second Esdras', in *The First and Second Books of Esdras* (M.A. Knibb and R.J. Coggins co-authors; Cambridge Bible Commentary; Cambridge: Cambridge University Press, 1979), pp. 76-305. The New English Bible's translation of 2 Esdras is supplemented with textual notes and comments on the more significant points.

J.M. Myers, *I and II Esdras* (Anchor Bible 42; Garden City: Doubleday, 1974). A translation with notes, supported by comments that paraphrase the text.

W.O.E. Oesterley, *2 Esdras (The Ezra Apocalypse)* (Westminster Commentaries; London: Methuen, 1933). A detailed commentary, although somewhat dated.

M.E. Stone, *Fourth Ezra* (Hermeneia; ed. F.M. Cross; Minneapolis: Fortress Press, 1990). Over twenty years in production, this is the standard 4 Ezra commentary, written by the foremost scholar in 4 Ezra studies.

B. Violet, *Die Apokalypsen des Esra und des Baruch in deutscher Gestalt* (Die griechischen christlichen Schriftsteller 32; Leipzig: Hinrichs Verlag, 1924). A classic commentary, if somewhat outdated.

List of Abbreviations

BZ	*Biblische Zeitschrift*
HTR	*Harvard Theological Review*
JBL	*Journal of Biblical Literature*
JSJ	*Journal for the Study of Judaism*
JSNT	*Journal for the Study of the New Testament*
JSNTSup	*Journal for the Study of the New Testament*, Supplement Series
JSP	*Journal for the Study of the Pseudepigrapha*
JSPSup	*Journal for the Study of the Pseudepigrapha*, Supplement Series
JTS	*Journal of Theological Studies*
NTS	*New Testament Studies*
ZAW	*Zeitschrift für die alttestamentliche Wissenschaft*
ZTK	*Zeitschrift für Theologie und Kirche*

1

INTRODUCTION

4 Ezra as 'Crisis of Faith' Literature

The text of 4 Ezra is first and foremost the literary testament to the religious struggle of one pious Jew long ago. For him, the messy currents of history had encroached upon and threatened to undermine a long-established trust in the sovereignty, justice and love of God. In the text that he left behind, he boldly examined the various components that had helped to form his religious perspective: religious traditions, scripture, worship, experience and intellect. All of these are thrown into the melting pot and stirred around, in the hopes that a new formulation might emerge that does justice to them all without neglecting or negating any of them. Whether or not he found the enterprise wholly successful is an issue that will be addressed in chapter 8 below.

4 Ezra can be said to belong to a literary genre of 'crisis of faith' literature, a genre whose contributors span time, culture and religion. Moreover, there are many more who have undergone a crisis of faith than simply those who have left a literary testament to that fact; the crisis of faith experiences of this silent multitude have gone unrecorded throughout history and today. If 4 Ezra is an ancient text from a foreign culture, it nonetheless witnesses to a phenomenon that is evident throughout the history of humanity in its quest for fulfilment.

Especially susceptible to critical re-examination is any theology that posits the existence of a transcendent creator who is characterized by power, love and justice; such a portrait is often difficult to defend in the light of the atrocities within history, over which the divine supposedly reigns. Much of this kind of re-examination has gone on within Jewish and Christian theological circles. This has been especially true since the mid-twentieth century in a post-Holocaust environment, when qualities of love, justice and sovereignty were often considered irreconcilable with a theological portrait of the God who reveals 'himself' in history (the masculine is used throughout wherever necessary, for convenience of style rather than theological correctness). Questions similar to those asked in 4 Ezra are asked by many today: Why are the lives of innocents torn apart by the instruments of oppression and injustice? Where is God's justice? Have the promises of God failed? Is the world running out of his control? Has he been overthrown by the forces of evil? Does he even exist any more, and if so, is he still up to the job? Has he simply grown tired, impotent, careless or unconcerned with the things of this world?

For some, these are the questions of those who are weak in faith, while for others these are the probings of theological giants. Whatever the case, the scriptures that the author of 4 Ezra cherished depict great men of faith grappling with similar kinds of issues. So, for instance, Job is shown to be a man of God, but one who refused to accept easy answers to his personal dilemma, answers that were common stock within his theological tradition but that failed to do justice to his own experiences and let God off the hook lightly and unaccountably. So too, the book of Psalms, the book of Hebrew prayers that have nurtured personal and communal faith throughout the ages, contains many examples not only of lament psalms but also of psalms of complaint against God. Moreover, in powerful imagery, Genesis 32 depicts Jacob, one of the great patriarchs of the Jewish people, wrestling with God, refusing to let him go until he (Jacob) was satisfied. Of course, Jacob was wounded in the struggle, but he was also transformed and renewed, deserving of a new name, Israel.

A similar account appears within the pages of 4 Ezra, as the author struggles with God, interrogating him in chapter after frustrating chapter, protesting against the God whose grand reputation fails to match his inability to sort out a desperate world. Just as the process was painful for the patriarch Jacob, so it proved to be the same for our author; and just as the process resulted in Jacob's transformation, so too it seems that the author of 4 Ezra emerged from his struggle and was transformed in his confidence in the justice, sovereignty and love of God. Whether in frustration or in confidence, his work is throughout a work of theodicy—that is, an attempt to understand and defend belief in the justice and sovereignty of God in view of the desperate condition of God's world. Some have thought that that matter is best addressed by means of philosophical and metaphysical enquiry—forms of 'objective', scientific deduction that can be replicated by anyone of any age. While the author of 4 Ezra does engage in some classic examples of logic, his is not a textbook on rational speculation and logical deduction. The main lines of his theodicy lie elsewhere, and are incorporated within a narrative that is noticeably marked out by the context of its day.

The Context of the Author's Theological Project

Theology is always contextual; the process of theological reflection does not come about without factors of cultural context impinging upon the agenda of one's concern, the manner of one's reflection, and the possibilities of one's lifestyle and action. Anyone who engages in a theological enterprise operates within the constraints of a historical context.

In this regard, however, 4 Ezra poses a significant problem, since the text reveals very little as to the specific situation out of which it arises. We are not told, for instance, some of the basic facts surrounding this text, such as the author's identity, his role and status, whether he belonged to a tightly-knit community or operated more freely within broader society, whom it was that he intended to influence with his text, or what the situation, attitudes and lifestyles were of his audience. Some of these matters will be considered in chapter 8 of this guide. For now, however, a less defined context can be outlined.

It appears that 4 Ezra can be dated at around the end of the first century CE. Although the main character of the text, Ezra, lived five centuries earlier, this is irrelevant to the issue of date, since the genre of apocalypse usually employs the technique known as pseudonymity, allowing the author to clothe his own identity in that of a hero from the past. The author is clearly writing after 70 CE, since the event that drives his inquest took place in that year: the destruction of Jerusalem by the military forces of the Roman empire.

The text may render a more precise dating by means of the imagery of chs. 11–12, which depicts a mighty eagle (symbolic of Rome) being crushed by a mighty lion (symbolic of the messiah). In the course of this long symbolic passage, we are shown three heads of the eagle that gain control of the whole earth through terrible power and oppress its people; the expectation of this passage is that the culmination of history will be within the reign of the third head. The behaviour of the eagle's three heads in 11.29-35 corresponds to what we know of the three

Roman emperors, Vespasian (69-79 CE), Titus (79-81 CE), and Domitian (81-96 CE), allowing this part of the text to be dated in Domitian's reign.

In line with this, the first verse of 4 Ezra begins with the words 'In the thirtieth year after the destruction of the city' (3.1). If this is an indication of the author's time of writing, we have further confirmation of 4 Ezra being a late first-century document (specifically, from about 100 CE). Many are hesitant, however, about using this verse for purposes of dating, since the author may simply be seeking to echo the opening words of the book of Ezekiel (1.1) in order to establish his own place in line with other post-destruction prophets of Israel's history. Nonetheless, the reference to the 'thirtieth year' may have some temporal significance, in corroboration of the general date arrived at by other means.

The location of the author at the time of writing is not clear from the text. Ezra is said to be situated in Babylon (3.1, 29), a symbolic reference to Rome. It may be, then, that the author wrote the text while living in Rome. There are problems with this view, however. Certain aspects of the text of 4 Ezra may suggest that the author was located in Judaea. The original text seems to have been written in a Semitic language (probably Hebrew), and shows considerable textual and theological relationship with 2 Baruch and (less evidently) with Pseudo-Philo and the Apocalypse of Abraham (despite some notable differences), all of which are almost certainly to be located within Judaea.

Probably, then, the references to Babylon in 3.1 and 3.29 do not signal the author's own location, but rather function as a pseudepigraphic device reinforcing the identity of the main character as Ezra, the priestly scribe depicted in the Jewish scriptures as one who left Babylon after the exile and established the Torah as the rule of life for the people of God in their own land. It may be, in fact, that the author considered the experience of living in a post-destruction context, even in Judaea, to be comparable to the experience of living in exile, far from the presence of Israel's God whose primary abode in the earthly sphere was the temple itself. To be removed from the temple is to be in exile, whether the exile is brought about by forceful removal of the people from the land or by forceful removal of the temple from the land.

Although I have cited only two aspects of the context out of which 4 Ezra comes, they are important aspects nonetheless. To locate 4 Ezra within Judaea late in the first century CE is to root it in a geographical centre of Jewish thought and practice at a formative period in Jewish self-definition. The destruction of Jerusalem had the potential to shatter the foundations of traditional Jewish theology, practice and piety, fixed as they were upon the very existence of the temple. In the wake of the events of 70 CE, Jewish leaders faced the task of considering the import of those events and what it meant to live faithfully before God in their new situation. This was a time of reconsidering the past in the light of the present, of re-evaluating what faithfulness to God entailed without recourse to the temple, of redefining how to live as the people of God gathered around the Torah.

The Jewish war against Rome resulted in more than the destruction of the temple and the city; after 70 CE, many of the Jewish groups and factions within Judaism disappeared as well. Of the Jewish factions mentioned by the Jewish historian Josephus, only Pharisaic Judaism seems to have emerged from the war relatively unscathed. Other groups within the umbrella of first-century Judaism were not so fortunate. The Sadducean influence deteriorated once their power-base in the temple was eroded, and we hear nothing more from Jewish sources about them. The Jewish freedom fighters who took action to overthrown the yoke of Roman domination, known as the Sicarii (named after the kind of knife they used) and the Zealots, seem to have disappeared relatively quickly. The covenant community at Qumran on the Dead Sea, thought to be a form of Essene Judaism, was destroyed in about 68 CE. But Pharisaic Judaism, which sought to replicate the purity of the temple within the everyday life of the people, was well situated to assist in the reformulation of Jewish life in a post-destruction context. In the Pharisaic programme, the essence of Jewish social and religious identity involved the embodiment of temple purity in all areas of life, especially in the home and in table fellowship. In this way, although the temple was a prominent symbol, their project did not require the existence of the temple itself. This left them well-placed to take a lead in the process of consolidating a new synthesis of Jewish identity in the post-destruction context.

The later Jewish rabbinic texts remember this reformulation period to have been overseen by one prominent leader, Yohanan ben Zakkai, who, according to the rabbinic literature from the third century and following, sought and was granted Roman approval to establish a school in the coastal city of Yavneh (sometimes known by its Greek equivalent, Jamnia), to the west of Jerusalem. There he gathered

prominent Jewish leaders together in an effort to contain the damage
after the temple's destruction and to salvage a Jewish way of life that
would take account of post-destruction realities. It is from this initiative
that Jewish rabbinic circles emerged.

It is likely that many elements in this tradition about the founding of
an academy at Yavneh are the product of later rabbinic idealization of
the period, as legendary elements crept into the tradition for theological and apologetic purposes. (So, for example, the tradition helps to
portray the roots of rabbinism as having Rome's seal of approval and
blessing.) The tradition also seems to grant the Yavnean rabbinic school
too exalted a place of importance in the early history of post-destruction Judaism, since a recognized, established and authoritative body of
teachers emerged over a much longer period of time and in a much
more complicated fashion than the tradition allows. Nonetheless, the
tradition is not simply legend without historical substance, and it is
likely that a group of post-destruction Jews came to live in Yavneh,
where they began teaching and addressing the needs of the post-
destruction Jewish community. Even if this process did not have the
significance that it came to have in later rabbinic literature, it nonetheless must even then have been recognizably notable as an important
feature in the reconstruction of Jewish life.

In this context of post-destruction Judaism, the view became more
and more prominent that sins could be atoned for, even without
recourse to the temple, by means of prayer, fasting and proper behaviour, all in loving dedication to God. Yohanan himself is remembered
in Jewish tradition as having declared that acts of loving-kindness will
atone for sin, just as sacrifices had earlier. In this way, even if some
sectors within the multi-faceted Judaism of the first century ceased to
exist after 70 CE, the destruction of the temple did not prove to be the
destruction of Judaism itself, but necessitated the reformulation of
Jewish life and faith before God.

The author of 4 Ezra breathed the same air of reformulation. The
text of 4 Ezra stands as the submission of one Jewish writer as he
sought to understand the implications of the temple's destruction for
the life of the people of Israel (see especially chapter 8 below).

The Genre and Text of 4 Ezra

At one point in the narrative, the author demonstrates an awareness of
standing in continuity with the apocalyptic prophet Daniel ('your

brother Daniel', 12.11). Just as the book of Daniel (or parts of it) is an apocalyptic writing, so the text of 4 Ezra belongs to the genre of 'apocalypse'. There has recently been much discussion about whether and how this genre can be defined. The general consensus would suggest a definition of this sort:

> an apocalypse is a narrative in which revelation is given to a human being by a divine being in order that earthly circumstances might be interpreted in the light of transcendent other-worldly and/or eschatological realities, thereby motivating its recipients to adopt certain beliefs and patterns of behaviour that are authorised by God.

A definition of this sort needs to be defined more closely for each individual apocalypse, since each one arises out of and addresses its own particular context. We have already seen something of the situation that gave birth to 4 Ezra: the destruction of the city of Jerusalem and its temple. The rest of this guide to 4 Ezra will consider the beliefs and patterns of behaviour that the author advocates as he explores that situation.

Every apocalyptic text that survives today from early Judaism is pseudonymous, a technique in which the author's own identity is cloaked in that of a famous religious hero of the past (this is not the case for the Christian biblical apocalypse, 'the Apocalypse of John' or 'Revelation'). The apocalypse of 4 Ezra, although written by a first-century Jew who is unknown to us, was transmitted down through the centuries not by Jews but by Christians. In its present form, it does not stand on its own but is part of a larger text called 2 Esdras ('Esdras' being the Greek form of the Hebrew name 'Ezra'), which is a composite of three texts. The long central section of 2 Esdras chs. 3-14 is where we now find the Jewish apocalypse 4 Ezra. On either side it, there appears two later Christian texts called 5 Ezra and 6 Ezra; these make up chs. 1–2 and chs. 15–16 (respectively) of 2 Esdras. (They are examined in chapter 9 of this guide.)

The terminology used in relation to 4 Ezra can often become confusing. Part of the problem arises from the fact that the text of 4 Ezra has survived in various sections of Christianity under various titles, sometimes being referred to as 2 Esdras, sometimes 3 Esdras, sometimes 4 Esdras (the full details appear in B.M. Metzger, 'The Fourth Book of Ezra', in *Old Testament Pseudepigrapha* [ed. J.H. Charlesworth; London: Darton, Longman & Todd, 1983, 1985], I, p. 516). It is standard today, however, to identify the text in the manner given above.

If the text has survived in Christian circles, it has survived in the
form of translations of the original which has long since been lost. The
textual history of 4 Ezra is complicated, but it is generally held that
4 Ezra was originally composed in Hebrew (Aramaic has also been
suggested, but there is little support for this today), even though the
Hebrew version has not survived. The Hebrew was translated into
Greek quite early on (4 Ezra 5.35, for instance, is quoted in Greek by
Clement of Alexandria late in the second century CE in *Stromateis*
3.16), although this version too has not survived. From the Greek
version come other translations that do survive: Latin, Syriac,
Georgian, Ethiopic, Armenian, Arabic and a fragment in Coptic.
Various other versions are also known, but they derive from these
earlier translations. It is generally maintained that the Latin text is the
most reliable, with the Syriac coming a close second.

Further Reading

1. *Brief studies on post-destruction Judaism*
J. Neusner, 'Judaism Beyond Catastrophe: The Destruction of the Temple and
    the Renaissance of the Torah', in his *Judaism in the beginning of Christianity*
    (London: SPCK, 1984), pp. 89-99. An interesting description of the effect
    of the temple's destruction on the Jewish community, showing various
    reactions, and contrasting the views of the apocalypticists with those of
    Yohanan ben Zakkai, who is depicted sympathetically as a relevant model
    of piety for all time.
L.I.A. Levine, 'Judaism from the Destruction of Jerusalem to the End of the
    Second Jewish Revolt: 70-135 CE', in H. Shanks (ed.), *Christianity and
    Rabbinic Judaism* (London: SPCK, 1992), pp. 125-49. A clear and concise
    overview of the period that demonstrates the effect of the destruction of
    the temple on Jewish life, the responses to this event made by various
    groups and key individuals, and the causes and aims of the Bar Kokhba
    revolt in 132-35 CE.

2. *Introductions to apocalyptic literature: monographs*
C. Rowland, *The Open Heaven* (London: SPCK, 1982). Following a thematic
    outline, Rowland considers what is meant by the term 'apocalyptic', its
    content, its origins, and its manifestations in early rabbinic Judaism and
    early Christianity.
J.J. Collins, *The Apocalyptic Imagination* (New York: Crossroad, 1987). A study
    of the apocalyptic genre and apocalypticism gives way to a chronological
    survey of the primary apocalyptic texts. (4 Ezra is studied on pp. 156-69.)

3. *Introductions to apocalyptic literature: articles*

C. Rowland, 'Apocalyptic: Scripture and the Disclosure of Heavenly Knowledge', in his *Christian Origins* (London: SPCK, 1985), pp. 56-64. Much good material packed into a concise and manageable introduction to the literature and its place within the world of early Judaism.

M.E. Stone, 'Apocalyptic Literature', in M.E. Stone (ed.), *Jewish Writings of the Second Temple Period* (Philadelphia: Fortress Press, 1984), pp. 383-441. An excellent survey of the origins of apocalyptic literature; its relation to prophetic and wisdom traditions; the major apocalypses; their primary features and purposes. An annotated bibliography appears at the end.

J.J. Collins, 'Genre, Ideology and Social Movements in Jewish Apocalypticism', in J.J. Collins and J.H. Charlesworth (eds.), *Mysteries and Revelations* (JSPSup 9; Sheffield: JSOT Press, 1991), pp. 11-32, esp. 11-25. A careful study of methodological issues relating to the genre 'apocalypse', their contents and contexts.

J.J. Collins, 'Apocalyptic Literature', in R.A. Kraft and G.W.E. Nickelsburg (eds.), *Early Judaism and its Modern Interpreters* (Philadelphia: Fortress Press, 1986), pp. 345-70. An extensive overview of general issues, showing trends and influences in scholarly study of the literature, followed by a helpful bibliography.

F.J. Murphy, *The Religious World of Jesus* (Nashville: Abingdon Press, 1991), pp. 163-67. A readable introduction to issues of terminology, the genre apocalypse, the 'apocalyptic worldview', the origins of Jewish apocalypticism, and the nature of apocalyptic discourse.

4. *The textual history of 4 Ezra*

M.E. Stone, *Fourth Ezra* (ed. F.M. Cross; Hermeneia Commentary; Minneapolis: Augsburg/Fortress Press, 1990), pp. 1-11. An extensive account of the textual history of 4 Ezra, as well as a consideration of date, location and original language.

A.F.J. Klijn, *Die Esra-Apokalypse (IV. Esra)* (Berlin: Akademie Verlag, 1992), pp. xi-xxx. A somewhat different account of the textual history of 4 Ezra to that of Stone. See too his earlier work, 'Textual Criticism of 4 Ezra: State of Affairs and Possibilities', in K.H. Richards (ed.), *SBL Seminar Papers 1981* (Chico, CA: Scholars Press, 1981), pp. 217-27.

2

ISSUES IN THE INTERPRETATION OF 4 EZRA

Structural Episodes and Character Dialogues

Whatever the disputed matters in 4 Ezra scholarship, two important aspects of this text are undisputed and provide the basis for understanding the text. Since the work of the German scholar G. Volkmar in 1863 (*Das vierte Buch Esrae* [Tübingen: Fues, 1863]), 4 Ezra is recognized to contain seven self-contained episodes (sometimes called visions). These seven units provide the foundation upon which the development of the narrative takes place, and appear as follows:

Episode I	4 Ezra 3.1–5.20
Episode II	4 Ezra 5.21–6.34
Episode III	4 Ezra 6.35–9.26
Episode IV	4 Ezra 9.27–10.59
Episode V	4 Ezra 11.1–12.51
Episode VI	4 Ezra 13.1-58
Episode VII	4 Ezra 14.1-48

Each episode is preceded, we are told, by a certain period of time (e.g. seven days, three days) in which Ezra is left in solitude before encountering the angel Uriel or God himself. (The period of solitude seems in 6.35 to be implied prior to episode I.) Episodes I to IV begin with a speech by Ezra before God, while episodes V to VII begin with a revelation from the divine side of the encounter through vision or theophany.

Episode IV is curious in that it begins in much the same style as the pattern already established in the previous three episodes, with Ezra initiating the episode, but it quickly takes on the revelatory character of the next three episodes. These structural considerations help to bolster the accepted view that episode IV is something of a pivotal point in the unfolding drama of 4 Ezra (see below, chapter 5). Already from these structural observations a second important feature of the text is obvious: its dialogical format. The text of 4 Ezra is dominated especially in the first three episodes by the back-and-forth debate of two primary characters, the prophet Ezra and his respondent, the angel Uriel. These two have little in common, at least on the theological issues that are under discussion in episodes I to III, and their lengthy discussions often frustrate the reader as much as they frustrate Ezra himself (see his final desperate cry in 9.14), since the characters seem to stand in deadlock over their fundamental views. They manage to cover various topics in their conversations, but pressing issues and concerns go unresolved, and neither character emerges as the victor in the dialogue. They fail to arrive at an agreed conclusion by the end of their dialogue proper in episode III, where they seem simply to agree to disagree.

The immediate consequence of this is obvious: when studying 4 Ezra, one needs always to be mindful of who is speaking at any given moment and of how a particular passage fits into the larger context of that character's theological stance. One cannot simply combine speeches uttered by Ezra with those uttered by Uriel in an effort to reconstruct some kind of a theology of 4 Ezra. To harmonize the two very different points of view held by the two characters in the early episodes is to undermine the tension that sustains the narrative of 4 Ezra and to unravel the tightly-knit theological web that the author has so subtly weaved. 4 Ezra is a complicated text that cannot be approached without regard for its dialogical format.

Besides the fact that the two main characters hold contrary views throughout a good deal of the narrative, a further factor warns the interpreter of 4 Ezra to proceed with caution. As the narrative progresses from the first three episodes into the second half of the book, the reader can observe a significant change in Ezra's character. Whereas in the first three episodes Ezra's demeanour is one of distress and complaint against God (3.1-36; 5.21-30; 6.38-59), the final episodes depict an Ezra who stands before God in reverent fear (10.25-37; 12.3b-9; 13.13b-20) and raises his voice in confident praise of God (13.57-58, in contrast to the insipid 'praise' offered by Ezra in 7.132-40, which is more a summons for God to live up to his merciful reputation). The Ezra of episode I is not the same as the Ezra of episode VII, where no trace remains of his earlier distress and trauma. As many have noted, Ezra's words in episode IV resemble the position advocated by Uriel throughout episodes I to III, a position that Ezra had found troublesome. Accordingly, scholars often speak of Ezra's 'conversion' in order to signify this change.

This brings us to the most critical issue in the study of 4 Ezra, the issue that has to be resolved in any interpretation of the book: What has happened to Ezra to allow for the transformation that we find in his character? First, however, one other matter needs consideration: the use of traditional source material within 4 Ezra.

The Author, his Sources and the Unity of 4 Ezra

Biblical scholarship in the late nineteenth and early twentieth centuries was alive with interest in source criticism—that is, determining where an ancient author might have used material already in existence (either oral or written) when producing his own text. 4 Ezra proved to be a text where such an approach had promise. The German scholar R. Kabisch was the first to apply source-critical methods to 4 Ezra (*Das vierte Buch Esra auf seine Quellen untersucht* [Göttingen: Vandenhoeck & Ruprecht, 1889]), followed later by the British scholar G.H. Box who followed Kabisch closely (*The Ezra-Apocalypse* [London: Pitman Press, 1912]).

In Box's view, the author of 4 Ezra made use of five pre-existing sources, which Box labelled S (the Salathiel apocalypse, so named because of Ezra's alias in 3.1), E (the Ezra apocalypse), A (the eagle vision), M (the Son of Man vision), and E2 (more Ezra material). Box located these sources within 4 Ezra in the following fashion:

S	most of chs. 3–10
E	4.52–5.13a, 6.13-29, 7.26-44, 8.63–9.12
A	most of chs. 11–12
M	most of ch. 13
E2	most of ch. 14

These five sources had been collected and assembled by a redactor (R) who was sympathetic to the distress expressed in S concerning the hope of personal and national salvation, and who found the solution to these matters in the age to come, when the wicked would be judged, evil would be destroyed, and all would be set right in a transcendent existence for those who were righteous in the present evil age. According to Box, since this solution (sometimes called a 'universal-transcendental eschatology') might have been viewed as inadequate in circles of traditional Jewish orthodoxy, the redactor included sections A and M, both of which depict God's salvific dealings on behalf of the nation Israel and the destruction of her wicked enemies (this solution is often called a 'national-earthly eschatology').

E2, which according to Box bestows upon apocalyptic texts a status equal to the canonical books, was also added in order to commend apocalyptic literature to the rabbinic school that, in his view, was hostile to the apocalyptic mind-set (a view that has subsequently been discredited).

In Box's handling of 4 Ezra, then, the redactor is concerned with matters relating to the salvation both of the individual and of the nation of Israel, and finds two kinds of solutions (universal and national eschatologies) in various sources known by him. Nowhere, however, does the redactor attempt to integrate these two solutions into a consistent viewpoint. Instead, he simply allows them to sit side by side in their new position within the somewhat disjointed text of 4 Ezra.

The sort of approach advocated by Box and others has some merit, since the author of 4 Ezra does seem to have made use of traditional material here and there in his text. Nonetheless, the approach is not without its weaknesses. The source-critical approach is dependent upon the criterion of 'inconsistency', since inconsistency of thought or concept within a text is considered to betray the existence of underlying sources. This raises the issue of the character of apocalyptic literature; in such literature, what counts as inconsistency?

M.E. Stone (among others) has addressed this issue, and in particular the 'two eschatology' approach to 4 Ezra taken by Box and others (*Features of the Eschatology of IV Ezra* [Atlanta: Scholars Press, 1989]; concise versions of Stone's case are found in his 'Coherence and Inconsistency in the Apocalypses: The Case of "The End" in 4 Ezra', *JBL* 102 [1983], pp. 229-43, and in his *Fourth Ezra*, pp. 204-207). He has shown conclusively that it is inappropriate to expect an apocalyptic text to be ordered in accordance with Aristotelian standards of logic, since the apocalyptic mind-set has no such expectations of itself. According to Stone, any inconsistencies discovered in 4 Ezra are not an embarrassment to the quality of the text, nor are they necessarily due to the existence of underlying sources. Instead, they are the natural result of variations in the context or subject matter. The author was not concerned with logical consistency in his eschatological descriptions, but used various eschatological ideas simply to support different points of argument at different places in his presentation. Stone has helped to demonstrate that it is inappropriate to impose categories of consistency upon an author who is not interested in satisfying our concerns in this regard, and whose chosen literary genre makes no such demands upon him. Stone's work discourages the kind of source-critical approach advocated by Box, Kabisch and others.

Another potential weakness of source-critical analysis is the danger that the task of interpretation is thought to be complete once the text is disassembled into fragments. One gets the impression from some source critics that the goal of interpretation is the dissection of a text into bits and pieces, leaving its various organs sitting lifeless after having discovered how they had been internally arranged. To continue the analogy, one needs also to ask about the life of the entity itself: how it moves, whether it hops, walks, or limps, its behaviour, its preferences, its idiosyncrasies. Box's approach does not advance much of an understanding of the overall unity of the text, and most scholars today have abandoned the extremes of a source-critical analysis in favour of a more holistic approach to the text. The one whom Box labelled the 'redactor' of 4 Ezra is today called the 'author', since there is little reason to doubt that the work came from a single individual whose work was his own as a single entity, despite the occasional inclusion of traditional material.

For this reason, most no longer find the task of interpretation to be the extraction of a handful of more ancient sources from the text of 4 Ezra. In seeking to do justice to the unity of the text, many have found one factor to be of special importance: an understanding of the person who composed the text as a statement of his religious struggle and conviction. It is to this kind of approach that we now turn.

The Author in Psychological Perspective

The earliest challenge to the source-critical approach of Kabisch and those who followed in his wake was mounted by the German form-critical scholar H. Gunkel in his 1891 review of Kabisch (in the journal *Theologische Literaturzeitung* 16.1, pp. 5-11). There, and later in his commentary on 4 Ezra ('Das vierte Buch Esra', in *Die Apokryphen und Pseudepigraphen des Alten Testaments* [vol. 2; ed. E. Kautzsch; Tübingen: Mohr, 1900], pp. 331-401), Gunkel sought to understand the text not in terms of a compilation of sources, but as a unity that testifies to the author's own personal dilemma. For Gunkel, a description of sources behind a text does not provide an explanation of the text itself. To understand 4 Ezra aright, one must take into account the psychological character of the author. Whereas source critics dismembered the text to discover its various component parts, Gunkel sought to work with the 'form' of the unified text as evidence of the author's purposes. Gunkel held that, in this regard, the dialogical format holds the key, for there the author had planted two aspects of his own self within the text, embodied in the characters of Ezra and Uriel. Each character personifies one aspect of the author's own psychological make-up, Ezra voicing his scepticism and Uriel voicing his faith. Throughout the first three episodes, the struggle between the two characters betrays the author's own dilemma, his tendency towards a split personality in matters of religion.

If Gunkel finds one set of issues addressed in episodes I to III, he finds another set in episodes IV to VI. The discussion of religious conundrums in the first three episodes gives way to the presentation of eschatological mysteries in the later episodes. If Ezra remains dissatisfied to the end of episode III, the eschatological depictions of episodes IV to VI grant him the assurance that God is in control of history. As a consequence, Ezra is lifted out of his despair. This, according to Gunkel, reflects the author's own psychological development. He finds resolution of his distress in the knowledge that God has charge over the world. The author's sense of dissatisfaction and anguish when religious matters are considered is abated through the depiction of the end when God will be shown to reign. For Gunkel, the author has not discovered any rational solutions to his existential dilemma; instead, he finds consolation in the conviction that his dilemma finds its resolution in the events of the future age.

The psychological approach introduced by Gunkel represents a step forward in 4 Ezra research. Gunkel's own views, however, while very influential, are open to question at places. He, like Box and others, makes much of what he considers to be two kinds of eschatology within 4 Ezra, a view that Stone's work reveals to be problematic, especially since no single passage in 4 Ezra contains either form of eschatological expectation in a self-contained, undiluted fashion. Moreover, the distinction between religious problems in episodes I to III and eschatological revelations in IV to VI seems rather artificial in itself and difficult to sustain from the text; some important issues addressed in the early episodes creep into the later episodes, while eschatological revelations are already present within the early episodes.

Contemporary scholarship on 4 Ezra is extremely indebted to Gunkel, and it is worth mentioning briefly a few scholars who have made important contributions in which Gunkel's influence is notice-able. In 1973, E. Breech argued that the author did not want to make specific theological points, but shaped his text to move from distress to consolation. It is this pattern, more than any concern to give proposi-tional solutions to religious problems, that primarily motivates the author ('These Fragments I Have Shored against my Ruins: The Form and Function of 4 Ezra', *JBL* 92, pp. 267-74).

Similarly, A.P. Hayman, while preferring not to speak of a psycho-logical disunity within the author, argued in a 1975 article that the text of 4 Ezra reveals the author's dissatisfaction with tradition Jewish theology, finding in its arsenal no adequate rational explanation for the problem of sin. Despite this, the author held out the hope of a future age in which Israel would be vindicated by God, and the power of this religious conviction overwhelmed any intellectual doubts ('The Problem of Pseudonymity in the Ezra Apocalypse', *JSJ* 6, pp. 47-56).

Hayman's ideas were developed further by his student A.L. Thompson in his PhD thesis, published in 1977. According to Thompson, in Ezra's attempt to understand how it is that God could allow the problem of evil to plague the whole of humanity, the author finds no rational explanation but nonetheless takes refuge from his anxiety in his confidence in the righteousness of God. 4 Ezra is the work of one whose attempt to make sense of a religious dilemma fails at the cognitive level, but whose experience bolsters his faith and trust in the God whose ways are beyond human comprehension (*Responsibility for Evil in the Theodicy of IV Ezra* [Missoula: Scholars Press]).

Finally, M.E. Stone has made much of this psychological interpreta-tion in his 1990 commentary on 4 Ezra, especially as Stone explains how the author moves from the early to the later episodes (*Fourth Ezra*; see also his 'Apocalypse' in 'Further Reading' below, and his earlier article, 'Reactions to Destructions of the Second Temple', *JSJ* 12 [1981], pp. 195-204). According to Stone, 4 Ezra is a testimony to its author's own spiritual pilgrimage; Ezra and Uriel embody two of the author's own inner impulses of grief and doubt on the one hand and of confident faith on the other. The primary dynamic within the text is the transformation of Ezra's 'religious consciousness', a transformation that does not come about by rational argument, but only by a profound overpowering conversion of his inner spirit, as depicted in episode IV.

It is apparent, then, that many have benefited from what Gunkel started by highlighting the psychological dynamic within the text.

4 Ezra is not to be treated simply as an encyclopaedia of theological ideas, and no interpretation can claim to be complete without an explanation of the psychological factors that have contributed to the shaping of the text.

With that said, however, this approach has the danger of quickly becoming reductionistic. The psychological approach runs the risk of reducing the theological import of 4 Ezra to merely the psychological level. The author's project does not simply operate at the psychological level of giving assurance and consolation, but includes also some propositional content, as a general theological perspective emerges from the narrative in relation to the theological problems considered throughout the first three episodes. If the psychological aspect is over-emphasized, the theological content may be missed. (This is the error of Breech's analysis, for instance, in which content is placed in a secondary position to the form of the text with its pattern of movement from distress to consolation.) Similarly, if the theological content is undervalued, we have little to fall back on except the psychological, which then becomes overblown. (This might have happened somewhat in Stone's otherwise excellent commentary.) Nonetheless, recognition of a psychological dynamic is of crucial importance to a proper understanding of 4 Ezra, and in this regard most contemporary scholarship on 4 Ezra is indebted to the work of Gunkel.

The Author in Relation to Gnostic Thought

Whereas Gunkel and many others consider Ezra and Uriel to represent two aspects of the author's inner life (e.g. scepticism and faith), the German scholar W. Harnisch accepts only the angel Uriel's voice as expressive of the author (*Verhängnis und Verheissung der Geschichte* [Göttingen: Vandenhoeck & Ruprecht, 1969]). Harnisch's approach is a development of an earlier suggestion by the German scholar E. Brandenburger, who went on to develop it further himself almost twenty years later (*Adam und Christ* [Neukirchen-Vluyn: Neukirchener Verlag, 1962]; *Die Verborgenheit Gottes im Weltgeschehen* [Zurich: Theologischer Verlag, 1981]). It takes as its starting point the conversion of Ezra within the narrative. It is undisputed that the Ezra who appears in the early episodes is not the Ezra of the later episodes, where Ezra advocates views that he had earlier rejected when spoken by Uriel. For Harnisch, then, it is the angel alone who speaks the mind of the author, since Uriel's perspective prevails in the end.

Working from Ezra's speeches in episodes I to III, Harnisch finds Ezra to voice a kind of heretical scepticism that shows affinity with some gnostic ideas growing up in the late first century that reflected a deficient understanding of the sovereignty of God. For Ezra, humanity is not accountable for its sinfulness since all are caught in the hands of fate by which their lives and the whole course of history is determined. According to Harnisch, this deterministic view of evil and sceptical view of God's powerful control is overruled at every point by Uriel, for whom the future age demonstrates God's sovereignty. Although the present age is corrupt, this is due to the sinfulness of humanity rather than the impotence of God. In the eschatological age, God's salvation will go to those who have been faithful to him through their obedience to the law. Harnisch postulates that Uriel's orthodox views were upheld by a community to which the author belonged, while Ezra's heretical views were advocated by the community's opponents. Little credence is given to the psychological approach of Gunkel and others, who identify the debates as representative of the author's own inner struggle; instead, for Harnisch, Ezra and Uriel are literary representatives of the theological differences of two distinct religious groups. As the narrative progresses, the author demonstrates that the position of his community's opponents is untenable, as Ezra is slowly won over to Uriel's position in the dialogues.

This interpretation of the text has not been well accepted. One of the first critics of it was A.P. Hayman ('Pseudonymity'), who demonstrated that Ezra's position in episodes I to III is not indebted to a gnostic influence at all; instead, it fits perfectly well within the context of orthodox Judaism. There is nothing heretical about Ezra's views. Harnisch fails to explain why the author chose Ezra as the exponent of a heretical threat to Jewish orthodoxy, when Jewish tradition held Ezra up as a great hero who had restored the law to the people and established the institution of the synagogue for the people to learn about and worship the true and living God. Ezra's arguments in the dialogues are admirable, and his determined attempt to understand the ways of God in a desperate situation both draws the reader sympathetically to identify with Ezra and has good precedent within the Jewish tradition. It is for reasons such as these that the interpretation set out by Harnisch has not won the day.

One might wonder, then, how it was the Harnisch could arrive at his interpretation. It appears that Harnisch has simply put his own particular interpretation on Ezra's speeches in his view that they advocate a sceptical determinism. It is true that Ezra does not paint much of an optimistic picture, because of his awareness of the power of sin and the impotency of humanity with respect to keeping the law. This is not, however, to concede that his views are representative of a gnostic heresy. Within the vast storehouse of Jewish theology, there is a strong tradition that recognizes the inadequacy of humanity before God and recognizes that salvation has nothing to do with the efforts of humanity but is effective only through the merciful initiative of Israel's gracious God. So, for instance, we repeatedly read in the Qumran scrolls sentiments such as this:

> Righteousness, I know, is not of man, nor is perfection of way of the son of man; to the Most High God belong all righteous deeds. The way of man is not established except by the Spirit which God created for him to make perfect a way for the children of men (1QH 7.29-32).

Examples of the same could be multiplied repeatedly (see, for instance, B.W. Longenecker, *Eschatology and the Covenant*, pp. 23-27.) The conviction expressed in this text from Qumran has close theological parallels to the speeches uttered by Ezra in the first three episodes, but no one accuses the Qumran author of abandoning Jewish orthodoxy for a gnostic heresy. The point he is making is the same that Ezra articulates throughout: salvation comes only by means of divine mercy, since all are guilty of sin before God and are unworthy of his saving grace.

The Author in Relation to Jewish Covenantal Thought

A crucial issue when studying 4 Ezra is the question of how the text is situated within the traditions and piety of Early Judaism. The modern discussion of this issue goes back to 1977, when the American scholar E.P. Sanders wrote his influential book *Paul and Palestinian Judaism* (Philadelphia: Fortress Press). One of Sanders's primary concerns was to undermine the scholarly belief that Early Judaism was permeated by a spirit of legalism. A legalistic interpretation of first-century Judaism finds it to have been an arid wasteland of human-centred religion, in which salvation was thought be earned through the performance of good works that were to outweigh one's bad works; in this form of religion, salvation could be analysed by a calculator. Missing is any emphasis on relationship with the living God who saves by his unmerited grace. This view of Early Judaism prevailed in Christian scholarly

circles at the time Sanders was writing, although it has progressively
fallen from favour since then.

Instead of this legalistic picture, Sanders supplies an understanding of
Judaism that Jewish scholars had long since commended to their
Christian counterparts, an understanding in which the key component
is the covenant. The awareness of a covenant relationship between
Israel and her God provided the scaffolding for the Jewish literature of
the period. The concern for proper behaviour in observance of the law
is obvious in Jewish texts, but this had little to do with earning
salvation by merit points, or with putting God under the obligation of
granting salvation to those who had proved themselves to be worthy of
it. What motivated pious Jews to obey the law was a concern to
preserve the covenant relationship that had already been established by
means of God's mercy upon Israel. God had been gracious to Israel in
establishing a special relationship of love with his people, a relationship
that, like all healthy relationships, requires both partners to act respon-
sibly in order to preserve and protect it. Judaism, throughout most of
its first-century forms, was not a legalistic but a covenantal religion, the
basis of which was the election of Israel by God, who had lovingly
chosen Israel to be his people and who in his mercy sustained this
relationship with them.

The speeches with which Ezra begins each of the first three episodes
of 4 Ezra are some of the best examples we have of the vitality of this
covenantal conviction within Early Judaism (3.1-36; 5.21-30; 6.35-59).
Moreover, Ezra is depicted as speaking the concerns of the people of
Israel after the destruction of the temple, all of whom, like Ezra, are
confused about how it could be that God would allow such intolerable
events to fall upon his beloved people (5.16-20; 12.40-45). This testifies to the kind of Judaism in which the author was immersed, and
gives added credence to Sanders's overall portrait of the covenantal
patterns that dominated most forms of Judaism in the first century.

When Sanders fits 4 Ezra into his picture of Early Judaism, however,
he finds it to be one of the few exceptions to the rule. For Sanders, like
Harnisch, it is not Ezra but Uriel who represents the author's position.
He finds Ezra to waver in his positions, while Uriel is consistent in his
viewpoint, advocating throughout a policy of legalistic perfectionism in
which salvation is bestowed upon those who are obedient to the law
without fault. This is the position to which Ezra eventually resigns
himself in episode IV. Sanders does not consider episodes V and VI to
be original to the text since they revive a nationalistic hope that plays

no part in Uriel's position; these episodes were added by a later redactor in order to bring the text into alignment with standard Jewish expectation. The same is true, says Sanders, of episode VII, which also was included to make the text more palatable to its Jewish audience. Although the later parts of the book may resurrect the hope of God's salvation for his people, they are nonetheless later additions to the text and run counter to the original author's intention (although Sanders has no evidence for suggesting this).

Sanders was not the first to take the view that 4 Ezra advocates a kind of legalistic 'piety'. He was, however, the first (at least to my knowledge) to suggest that the legalism of 4 Ezra was exceptional within the Judaism of his day. Prior to Sanders's work on Judaism, whenever 4 Ezra was interpreted as advocating a kind of legalism, it was seen as characteristic of the general ethos of Early Judaism, held in the unfortunate grip of self-reliance in a programme of works-righteousness. If Sanders's work on the covenantal structure of most forms of Judaism is correct, and if 4 Ezra does advocate a kind of works-oriented, legalistic perfectionism, then 4 Ezra does not stand as a specimen of the typical piety of Early Judaism but as an exception, an oddity, a distinctive and unique text in what it proposes.

There are many interpreters who would dispute a legalistic reading of 4 Ezra, finding the author's interests to lie elsewhere. For many, 4 Ezra is an expression of covenant theology, articulating complete confidence in God's sovereignty in this world and faithfulness to his people Israel. It stands as a monument to the spirit of expectant faith in God, even when rational attempts to comprehend this world fail.

So it seems that there are divergent streams of thought on the matter of 4 Ezra's relationship to traditional covenantal patterns of thought in Judaism. In general, scholars tend to hold one of three possible views: (1) 4 Ezra ultimately supports a kind of covenantal framework in which God's gracious faithfulness to ethnic Israel is assured in the end, even if it looks suspect in the present; (2) 4 Ezra redefines traditional covenantalism, narrowing the scope of divine grace and thereby limiting covenant membership to include only a remnant, a much smaller group than the whole of ethnic Israel; (3) 4 Ezra breaks out of traditional covenantal confidence in God's faithfulness to corporate Israel and postulates another concept of the ways of God, in which salvation is a matter of the efforts of each individual in order to overcome sin and to amass works of righteousness in one's favour before God. Perhaps these approaches can be entitled 'covenantal confirmation', 'covenantal

redefinition', and 'covenantal abrogation' respectively. A discussion of
this matter appears later in this guide (see chapter 8 below).

In the end, of course, discussion of scholarly developments in 4 Ezra
scholarship can help to shed light on important issues relating to the
text, but it cannot be a substitute for immersing oneself in the text of
4 Ezra itself, to which we turn our attention now.

Further Reading

1. *Detailed reviews of the history of 4 Ezra scholarship*
A.L. Thompson, *Responsibility for Evil in the Theodicy of IV Ezra* (Missoula:
    Scholars Press, 1977), pp. 85-107. A thorough and helpful chronological
    survey from 1863 to 1974.
E. Brandenburger, *Die Verborgenheit Gottes im Weltgeschehen: Das literarische und
    theologische Problem des 4. Esra Buches* (Zurich: Theologischer Verlag,
    1981), pp. 22-57. An extensive thematic review of primary issues and
    major contributors.
M.E. Stone, *Fourth Ezra* (Minneapolis: Fortress Press, 1990), pp. 11-21. Stone
    organizes his survey around issues of sources and literary unity, touching
    on the more important contributors to 4 Ezra scholarship in these matters.
B.W. Longenecker, *Eschatology and the Covenant: A Comparison of 4 Ezra and
    Romans 1-11* (JSNTSup 57; Sheffield: JSOT Press, 1991), pp. 40-49. A
    chronological survey of major contributors, with a fuller treatment than
    can be offered here.

2. *On the unity of 4 Ezra*
M. Knowles, 'Moses, the Law and the Unity of 4 Ezra', *NovT* 31 (1989), pp.
    257-74. Knowles demonstrates that a chronological framework of forty
    days weaves through the text from start to finish, as a means of establishing
    Ezra's identity in relation to Moses.
M.E. Stone, 'On Reading an Apocalypse', in J.J. Collins and
    J.H. Charlesworth (eds.), *Mysteries and Revelations* (JSPSup 9; Sheffield:
    JSOT Press, 1991), pp. 65-78. The criterion for unity is not necessarily
    logical consistency but coherence, a notion that may involve the author's
    own personality and experience as the primary unifying factor.

3. *Helpful bibliographies on 4 Ezra appear in*
J.H. Charlesworth, *The Pseudepigrapha and Modern Research, with a Supplement*
    (Chico, CA: Scholars Press, 1976/81), pp. 113-16, 284-86.
A.F.J. Klijn, *Die Esra-Apokalypse (IV.Esra)* (Berlin: Akademie Verlag, 1992),
    pp. xxxi-xxxv.

3

EZRA'S INITIAL SPEECHES

Ezra and his Distress

Each of the first three episodes begins with Ezra taking the initiative to direct his concerns towards God. So in 3.1, his alias is Salathiel, which in its Hebrew form (s'lty'l) may be understood to mean 'I have asked of God'. His tortured mental state is clearly indicated in each of these initial speeches. In the first episode, Ezra is troubled as his thoughts rise up in his heart (3.1), and his spirit is greatly agitated (3.3), causing him to speak 'anxious words' to God (3.3). The second episode begins the same way, with grief rising up again in Ezra's heart (5.21), leading him to deliver his speech before God (5.22). The third episode resembles the first two, Ezra weeping (6.35) as his heart is troubled again (6.36), his spirit is greatly aroused, and his soul is in distress (6.37). So, of course, Ezra speaks once again to God. Even the fourth episode, which functions as the turning point of the story, begins as do the initial three, with Ezra's heart being troubled yet again (9.27), resulting in his final self-initiated speech to God (9.28).

The grief felt by Ezra is not difficult to understand, and is explained clearly right from the start, being caused by the 'destruction of the city' (3.1), the 'desolation of Zion' (3.2). Each of the three initial speeches explores the ramifications of this disastrous event, seeking to understand how it might be that God could allow such a situation.

We can appreciate the poignancy of Ezra's heartache all the more by recognizing the central role that Jerusalem and the Jerusalem temple (= Zion) played within Jewish society. Although most of the Jewish population of the first century were scattered beyond the boundaries of the land of Israel, Jerusalem and its temple would have remained dear to the heart of the vast majority of Jews. Pilgrimages to Jerusalem were highlights in the life of a pious Jew, and a tax was collected throughout the Jewish population in order to alleviate the heavy costs of maintaining the temple and the worship that took place there (cf. Neh. 10.33-34; Exod. 30.11), including sacrifices made every day for the sins of the Jewish people collectively. Prayers were directed towards the city of Jerusalem (cf. 1 Kgs 8.29-30; Dan. 6.10), understood even then as the *axis mundi*, the centre or navel of the world where heaven and earth meet (called 'the navel of the earth' in Ezek. 38.12; cf. Ezek. 5.5; Jub. 8.19; Sib. Or. 5.248-50). Although God's presence could not be restricted to a certain geographical region (he was, after all, the one who sustained the whole of creation), nonetheless on earth he had chosen for himself a dwelling place *par excellence* on Mount Zion, the temple mount, in the midst of his people (cf. Mt. 23.21).

But the temple was not just a religious symbol; it functioned as the centre and focus of important aspects of Jewish society—economic, political, religious, scholastic. Many aspects of Jewish life and culture met at Jerusalem where they were intricately intertwined. The destruction of Jerusalem would have seriously disrupted the normal workings of first-century Jewish society, especially in Judaea. This all-encompassing cultural catastrophe provoked a reconsideration of God's relationship to that society, just as it had on the part of the post-exilic prophets after the first destruction of the temple in 586 BCE. The same concerns motivate Ezra here in 4 Ezra.

One might expect that, in the case of a breakdown in the covenant relationship between God and his people, an examination of the situation would reveal a flaw on the side of the people. Traditionally, whenever disastrous events struck the people of Israel, retrospective analysis laid the blame at the feet of the people, who had proved themselves to be disobedient to God and who had brought God's punishment upon themselves. Ezra, however, does not adhere to such a view, at least not in the first episodes of 4 Ezra. There, Ezra reveals what he perceives to be a flaw on the divine side of the relationship.

This is especially evident in Ezra's initial speeches. These deserve close attention, not simply because they are some of the more interesting parts of the text, but because they establish the context of Ezra's passionate concerns.

Ezra's Initial Speech in Episode I

Ezra's initial speech in 3.4-36 comprises four major parts. In the first and second (3.4-11, 12-19) Ezra recalls aspects of the character of God as revealed in history, while in the third and fourth (3.20-27, 28-36) Ezra puts on the mantle of prosecutor in a damaging assessment of God in the light of the description of God given already in the first two parts of the speech.

In 3.4-19, Ezra rehearses some of the primary events from creation to the giving of the law to Israel. 3.4-11 recalls the formation of Adam by God, Adam's transgression, the manner in which sin permeated the ways of humanity, the destruction of the inhabitants of the world, and the rescue of one who was righteous, Noah. Ezra has done little else than reconstruct the general threefold pattern of Genesis 1–11: (1) Divine action results in life and prosperity, (2) human action results in sinfulness, and (3) human sinfulness results in divine punishment. 3.12-19 carry on the emphases of Genesis, now moving into the covenantal history of Genesis 12 and beyond. God chose for himself Abraham, whom he loved and with whom he made 'an everlasting covenant' (3.15) that would benefit the (true) descendants of Abraham forever. Ezra highlights the two great events of Israel's early history: the exodus out of Egypt and the giving of the law. The latter is described in 3.18-19 in dramatic imagery:

> You bent down the heavens and shook the earth, and moved the world, and caused the depths to tremble, and troubled the times [or better: 'and troubled creation']. Your glory passed through the four gates of fire and earthquake and wind and ice, to give the law to the descendants of Jacob, and your commandment to the posterity of Israel.

The flair and ceremony in this magnificent description of the cosmological significance of God's giving of the law to Israel far exceeds Ezra's rather lack-lustre description of God's creative activity at the beginning of time in 3.4-5. The reader now expects to hear of grand things as a consequence.

Instead, however, we hear a disastrous tale, a divine comedy of errors. Despite God's display and pageantry in giving the law, he has overlooked the one thing necessary if the law is to be obeyed: he has allowed the 'evil heart' to remain in his people (3.20). With this, Ezra's tone changes from that in 3.4-19, as he becomes the accuser of God. Ezra's point throughout 3.20-27 is that Israel's sinfulness, which is no different from that of Adam, is due to a prior error on the part of God, who did not root out evil in the heart of the people. As a result, Israel stands no chance of obeying the law. The end result is that, ironically, the city that bore God's own name (3.24) has been delivered by God

into the hands of God's own enemies (3.27). The grand description of
the giving of God's law to those who would obey it has collapsed into
a mournful description of the giving of God's city to those who oppose
his ways.

Ultimately Ezra's charge here calls into question the sovereignty of
God, since God's own law, given to Israel in the midst of cosmic
splendour, is shown to be no match for the power of sin within the
human heart. But Ezra has more in store in his critique of God's ways,
for in 3.28-36 he goes further by calling into question the justice of
God. This is accomplished simply by comparing the state of Babylon
with that of Israel. The sins of Babylon are immense, and yet it
prospers; Israel, however, whose sin is far less significant, is crushed
underfoot by Babylon, with divine approval.

This state of affairs runs precisely contrary to the ways of God
described by Ezra in 3.4-11. There Ezra recounts how 'the inhabitants
of the world' who scorned God were destroyed by God for their
sinfulness, while Noah was saved by God because of his righteousness.
If this precedent is applied to Ezra's situation, Babylon, which has been
unmindful of the commandments of God (3.33), stands in the place
equivalent to the sinful inhabitants of the world (described in 3.8-10),
while Israel, which has trusted in God's covenant (3.32) and has
observed his commandments far better than any other nation (3.35),
should stand in the place equivalent to the righteous Noah (described
in 3.11). Here is a discrepancy between the characterization of God
found in the sacred books of Judaism (as recalled by Ezra in 3.4-11) and
the characterization of God at present—a God who tolerates those who
are evil and allows them to prosper at the expense of those who are his
people (3.30) and endeavour to obey him. The God depicted in scripture, who acts to destroy the unrighteous and rewards the righteous, is
not evident to Ezra from the events of recent history. Ezra does not
hesitate to highlight this incongruity in the activity (or non-activity) of
God.

This first speech is one of the most daring criticisms of God in any
religious text. Ezra pulls no punches, and refuses to hold back in his
accusations against God. There is no sense of watering down his
charges out of respect for God. The fact that the culprit is the divine
creator does not lessen the charges; in fact, it heightens their significance. In Ezra we have a figure who speaks his mind honestly and
boldly without fearing recriminations, who has neither praise for God
nor reproach for his people. The end of the episode depicts Ezra as the

one who speaks on behalf of Israel in presenting a defence to God (see Phaltiel's words in 5.16-18), but the initial speech of Ezra depicts more than a defender of Israel; Ezra has shown himself to be a formidable prosecutor of God himself. It was the eighteenth-century philosopher Immanuel Kant who said that even God 'must be compared with our ideal of moral perfection before he can be recognised as such' (*Foundations of the Metaphysics of Morals* 2), a sentiment similar to that of Ezra in his interrogations of God seventeen hundred years earlier.

Ezra's Initial Speech in Episode II

Ezra's opening speech in episode II plays on the same themes developed already in episode I, but this speech is much less sophisticated and does little to progress beyond what Ezra has already argued. The emphasis in 5.23-27 is, as in 3.12-19, on the election of Israel by God's covenant grace, reinforced through eight images of election. As in 3.18-19, the giving of the law to 'this people whom you have loved' is depicted in 5.27 as the validation *par excellence* of that relationship. Ezra's complaint is found briefly in 5.28-30, where he follows the argument already delineated in 3.28-36: Israel, described as 'your only one', 'your people' who have 'believed [or better: 'trusted in'] your covenants', has been humiliated and scattered by those who oppose the ways of God.

Ezra's simple speech illustrates a discrepancy between the people's chosen status and their present condition. In Ezra's view, this discrepancy reveals a possible inconsistency in the ways of God, who has shown himself in the past to love Israel as the apple of his eye, but now seems to have lost his first love. If there is little progress from the first speech of episode I, this may be precisely the point; Ezra's distress remains unresolved and he is back where he started.

Ezra's Initial Speech in Episode III

Ezra's speech here has, like that in episode I, been very skilfully composed. Although less complicated than that of episode I, it nonetheless makes its point with telling force and focused accuracy. A long section first recounts the description in Genesis 1 of God's activity in the seven days of creation (6.38-54, although the seventh day of rest is not mentioned). This comes to bear on Ezra's concern for Israel in 6.55-59, where he puts forward an argument based on a traditional Jewish correlation between Adam and Israel: just as Adam was given dominion over the earth, so Israel is expected to stand in Adam's place as the earthly viceroy of God. But Ezra contrasts the dominion of Adam, whom God appointed as the ruler over all that he had made (6.54), with the lowly state of Israel, which is at the mercy of all (6.57-59). Dominion is not granted to Israel, for which the world was created (6.55, 59), but to those who oppose God's people. By means of this line of argument, Ezra demonstrates that God's plans for creation were meant to culminate in the establishment of Israel's regency over the other nations of the world, and concludes that these divine plans have been thwarted.

As in the initial speech of episode I, Ezra is not simply calling into question God's faithfulness to Israel. He has struck deeper by undermining confidence in the sovereignty of God in the affairs of the world. This is accomplished especially well in the way Ezra depicts the relationship between God's creative word and his resulting work. Ezra demonstrates that the things that God 'commanded' and 'said' in the events of creation came to be; as he says, 'Your word accomplished the work' (6.38), and 'Your word went forth, and at once the work was done' (6.43). Conversely, however, the things that God 'said' in relation to Israel have failed to take place. God's powerful word in the events of creation contrasts with God's impotent word with respect to Israel. If God's word concerning Israel has come to nothing, his authority in the affairs of this world is called into question. If Israel's God fails to act on their behalf as he has said he will do, it may be due to his own impotence. The test case of God's cosmic sovereignty is focused on the condition of Israel, a test that God appears to have failed.

In this episode, as in the two previous ones, Ezra shows himself to be unfaltering in his courageous attack on God's reputation (second perhaps only to the devastating critique of God offered by Ivan in Fyodor Dostoyevsky's *The Brothers Karamazov*). Throughout these initial speeches, Ezra has called into question central aspects of God's character, such as the adequacy of his sovereignty, his justice, his love. These aspects are precisely those that have been the subject of much theological consideration in the aftermath of the holocaust since the mid-twentieth century. Ezra's reassessment of God's character and reputation may not be as developed as that of modern thinkers, but it stands as an early monument to the sense of justice inherent in the human spirit, a sense that cannot be satisfied until all is set aright, no matter who the offender or how exalted the status. Justice knows no bounds and excludes no one, not even the creator of the universe.

The Case against Human Ability to Understand God's Ways

If the final point made above stirs up grand aspirations in the human soul, it itself is quickly called into question by the angel Uriel, in response to Ezra's first two initial speeches. The debate between Ezra and Uriel focuses on the ability of human reason to comprehend the ways of God. As was the case with Ezra's initial speeches, the more profound and interesting version of the debate is found in episode I rather than in episode II, which is largely just a truncated version of its earlier twin. Here, then, only the debate in episode I will be examined.

Uriel, who first appears in 4 Ezra at 4.1, makes his case immediately, stating explicitly that Ezra cannot hope to understand God's ways (4.2). Ezra, as bold as ever, insists that he can (4.3; cf. 4.5). Uriel propounds a series of riddles that Ezra cannot answer (4.5-9) as a means of making his initial point again (4.10-11). This leads Ezra to protest in desperation that life is devoid of all meaning if it is reducible to suffering without the possibility of understanding why suffering exists or what purpose it serves (4.12). Uriel employs another intriguing parable to reinforce his point that human understanding can only go so far before trespassing its proper boundaries (4.13-21). When he urges Ezra to seek understanding about the things of earth rather than the things of heaven, Ezra retorts that that is precisely what he has been doing! His concern has been to understand the things of this world: why Israel, the people loved by God, has been forsaken; why the law and the covenant are to no avail; and what God intends to do about it all (4.22-25). These matters are, in Ezra's view, susceptible to human investigation, and he feels he has the right to enquire about them without overstepping the boundaries of reason.

In many ways, this debate concerning the nature and boundaries of human rationality parallels the debates within early seventeenth-century Christianity concerning the relationship between religion and science (compare the controversy between Galileo and the church authorities), and Ezra's viewpoint might have been looked upon with kind regard by those who, in the spirit of the Enlightenment, sought for the Kantian ideal of religion within the bounds of reason.

Within the text of 4 Ezra itself, the importance of this debate cannot be overemphasized. The two characters are shown to be at loggerheads: each one approaches the issues raised in Ezra's initial speech with his own point of view concerning the ways of God, and their respective views are incompatible. Most importantly, it is significant that

Ezra's attempts to understand the ways of God operate from a traditional covenantal framework, seeking to comprehend his situation in
the light of Israel's position as God's covenant people. Uriel, however,
maintains that human wisdom cannot hope to comprehend the ways of
God, the implication being that this may be the case even if that
wisdom arises out of a conventional awareness of the covenantal relationship between God and his people. In Uriel's point of view, Ezra's
manner of considering the ways of God is misguided, and if Ezra's
vantage point is improper, so too is his understanding. Uriel's point of
view is a potential threat to Ezra's traditional expectations of the
covenant, and is one of which we will see more as the argument
unfolds. Before looking at Uriel's position in more detail, however, we
need to examine one other aspect of Ezra's position, as evident in his
initial speeches: that is, his view of the gentiles.

Ezra's Attitude toward the Gentile Nations

For both historical and theological reasons, it is important to make brief
mention of Ezra's attitude toward the gentile nations, as depicted most
clearly in episode III. Whereas Israel is said to be 'chosen' by God
(6.54) and identified as God's people 'whom you have called your first-
born, only begotten, zealous for you, and most dear' (6.58), other
nations are despised as 'nothing', compared to 'spittle', and are said to
be as significant to God as 'a drop from a bucket' (6.56).

This attitude, which is strikingly problematic to the 'progressive'
modern mind, is not without parallel in the literature of Early Judaism.
It follows on not from some self-congratulatory sense of smug self-
righteousness, but from an understanding of the people of Israel as
God's elect, who have been given and observe God's commandments.
Consequently they can be described as 'a race of most righteous men'
(Sib. Or. 3.219), having been blessed 'above the nations' (Pss. Sol.
11.9; cf. 11.8-11; Ps. Philo 11.1; 19.8; 30.4; 35.2). Conversely, the
gentiles, who do not possess the law (cf. Pss. Sol. 17.24; Ps. Philo
10.2), can be described as 'sinners' (Pss. Sol. 17.15). The double charge
that gentiles are like 'spittle' to God and as significant to him as a drop
of water (cf. Isa. 40.15) is found in two other Jewish works, both
roughly contemporary with 4 Ezra (Ps. Philo 7.3; 12.4; 2 Bar. 82.5). A
passage like Jub. 22.16 is especially poignant in its attitude towards the
gentiles:

> Separate yourselves from the gentiles, and do not eat with them, and
> do not perform deeds like theirs. And do not become associates of
> theirs, because their deeds are defiled, and all of their ways are conta-
> minated, despicable and abominable.

Similarly, Pseudo-Philo cites idolatry as the primary characteristic of
the gentile nations, the sin that provokes all other sins (Ps. Philo 27;
44). Accordingly, that author encourages Israel to avoid mingling with
pagan nations (e.g. 21.1; 34.1-5; 44.7; 45.3).

These brief comments demonstrate the manner in which an awareness of Israel's elected state facilitated within Jewish piety a further
sense of nationalistic distinctiveness, of cultural separation, and, in some
cases at least, of ethnic superiority. (For more on this, see Longenecker,
Eschatology, pp. 27-31). In his initial speech of episode III, Ezra is
shown to share in this conviction, arising as it does from an awareness
of God's covenant relationship with Israel. It is precisely this awareness,
however, that is held up to interrogation and re-examination in the
light of Uriel's position, to which we now turn.

Further Reading

For studies on Ezra's theological concerns, see the 'Further Reading'
list at the end of chapter 4.

1. *On the importance of the temple within early Judaism*

E.P. Sanders, *Judaism: Practice and Belief, 63 BCE–66 CE* (London: SCM Press;
   Philadelphia: Trinity Press International, 1992), pp. 47-76. A detailed
   description of the temple and its role within early Judaism.

N.T. Wright, *The New Testament and the People of God* (London: SPCK, 1992),
   pp. 224-26. A brief and readable study, highlighting the theological and
   social significance of the temple.

C. Rowland, *Christian Origins* (London: SPCK, 1985), pp. 39-41. A brief and
   readable study, highlighting primarily the social significance of the temple.

J.D. Levenson, *Sinai and Zion* (Minneapolis: Winston Press, 1985), pp. 11-84.
   A fascinating theological sketch of the centrality and importance of Zion.

2. *On the covenantal pattern within most forms of early Judaism*

E.P. Sanders, *Paul and Palestinian Judaism* (Philadelphia: Fortress Press, 1977). A
   book that acts as the watershed for the contemporary study of Judaism,
   despite its somewhat two-dimensional depiction of the Jewish 'pattern of
   religion'. The first part of the book examines important 'Palestinian' literature, interpreting it as evidencing a pattern of 'covenantal nomism'. See
   further his *Judaism* (cited above), pp. 241-78.

N.T. Wright, *The New Testament and the People of God*, pp. 244-79. Roots
    Jewish covenantalism within the broader framework of Jewish theological
    convictions concerning monotheism and eschatology.

J.D.G. Dunn, *The Partings of the Ways* (London: SCM Press; Philadelphia:
    Trinity Press International, 1991), pp. 18-36. Speaks of four pillars of early
    Judaism: monotheism, election of the covenant people, the torah, and the
    land.

B.W. Longenecker, *Eschatology and the Covenant*, pp. 14-33. A survey of schol-
    arly perceptions of 4 Ezra's relation to covenantal theology is followed by
    a portrait of Jewish covenantalism in its basics and its diversity.

C. Rowland, *Christian Origins*, pp. 25-28. A concise and readable
    presentation.

4

THE HEART OF
THE MATTER

Uriel's Position in Episodes I and II

If Ezra's position is clear from the beginning, Uriel's position unfolds gradually throughout the first three episodes. In fact, the first two episodes give us little content from Uriel, except for a basic skeleton upon which he puts flesh in episode III.

That skeleton is evident first in his words in 4.26-27, where he directs Ezra's consideration to the next age; the righteous have nothing to hope for in the present age:

> The [present] age is hurrying swiftly to its end. It will not be able to bring the things that have been promised to the righteous in their appointed times, because this age is full of sadness and infirmities.

This, as he goes on to explain in 4.28-32, is due to the evil seed that was sown in Adam's heart and that must yield its evil produce prior to the time of harvest threshing. Although it can be neither rushed nor delayed (4.33-43), the end may be soon to appear (4.44-52). Uriel then relates an account of what the end of the present age will be like, an account that most think the author has taken from an older apocalyptic source in order to fill out Uriel's position (5.1-13). It depicts a wholly atrocious time of cosmological disruption, deformity and chaos, when righteousness disappears and unrighteousness flourishes. This is the extent of Uriel's position in episode I.

In episode II, Uriel's position does not progress much beyond that in episode I. As in episode I, the debate about human understanding gives way to a discussion in which Uriel's eschatological agenda takes pride of place throughout the second half of the episode. The eschatological focus is introduced by Uriel at 5.40b, and Ezra immediately picks up

on it by postulating three ways in which God's dealings prior to the
eschaton might have been improved, all of which are ruled out by
Uriel (5.41-55). The discussion continues, as Ezra learns more: first,
that God himself will bring about the end of the present age, the right-
ness of his ways thereby being proven on the other side of the eschatological boundary (5.56–6.6); second, that there will be no interval
between the ages (6.7-10), a claim that runs against the eschatological
depiction given by Uriel in (for instance) 7.26-44, and reminds us that
the apocalyptic genre does not demand consistency in this regard (see
above, chapter 2); and third, that the horrific events at the end of this
age (6.18-24) will be followed by an age of God's salvation (6.25-28),
when evil will be overthrown, truth will be revealed, and 'the heart of
the earth's inhabitants shall be changed and converted to a different
spirit' (6.26). All that Ezra pleads for in the present will become
manifest only in this period in the unfolding of the ages.

If Uriel's position in episode II does not progress much beyond that
in the first episode, some advance is evident nonetheless. If in episode I
Uriel depicted the future age as redressing the evils of this age, this
functioned as more of a theoretical assurance, without much to
substantiate it. In episode II, however, Uriel's assurance is filled out,
especially in the concluding depiction of the end of the age (6.18-28).
As the description of the end is given to Ezra by means of a great
supernatural voice that sounded like the flow of many waters (6.13, 14,
17), the place where he was standing is shaken, symbolizing the trem-
bling of the foundations of the earth since they know that they too will
be transformed in the end (6.14-16, 29). Such an experience would no
doubt lend significant reinforcement to Uriel's words, granting Ezra
substantiation of Uriel's eschatological orientation in a way that is
lacking in episode I.

Prior to being told about the events of the end of the age, Ezra, who
seems up to this point to have been lying on his bed (cf. 3.1), is
instructed to rise to his feet the proper position for one who is having
the events of God's eschatological triumph revealed to him. (Ezra rises
to his feet in 4 Ezra only at significant points in the narrative: 4.47;
6.13, 17; 7.2; 10.33; 13.57; 14.2.) Much in the way that Christian
audiences at a full performance of Handel's Messiah rise for the singing
of the Hallelujah Chorus, with its magnificent acclamation 'And he
shall reign forever and ever', so too Ezra rises as he hears about the
ultimate victory of God over evil to the benefit of those who have
been faithful to him.

In this regard, it is interesting to note that many scholars consider the eschatological description in 5.1-13 at the end of episode I to be the first half of a traditional apocalyptic source, the second half of which appears at the end of episode II in 6.18-28 (a view similar to that of early source critics who cited both as being part of the source they identified as E; see above, chapter 2). This might be significant, since the first half of the source is depressing in its depiction of faithlessness, corruption and perversity, while the second half of the source depicts the pervasiveness of evil being overthrown by a righteous and sovereign God.

Before considering Uriel's position as it is unveiled in episode III, mention should be made of Uriel's statement in 5.40 (spoken on behalf of God) which assures Ezra that the end towards which God is working is one that will benefit his people whom he loves: 'You cannot discover my judgement, or the goal of the love that I have promised to my people.' Ezra, no doubt, accepts this to be good news for those whom he represents, the nation of Israel, and Uriel does nothing to frustrate this impression. Nonetheless, a word of caution needs to be registered at this point, since there is more to Uriel's case than is presented in the first two episodes. In episode III, the term 'Israel' itself seems open to redefinition, as the identity of God's people is reconsidered. As Uriel's position develops throughout episode III, there will be much to displace the traditional hope for the salvation of ethnic Israel, at least as Ezra was formulating it. The issue will become not simply 'Which age will Israel possess?', but more fundamentally, 'Who will constitute Israel in the next age?'

Uriel's Position Clarified in 7.1-18

Episode III is an extremely long section of the book, partly because it is here where the dialogue moves to a new level of debate, encompassing new matters not considered to any extent earlier.

After Ezra's initial speech, Uriel responds (without the debate on the limits of human understanding that typified the earlier episodes) with analogies that contrast the burden and toil of the present age with the splendour of the next age (7.1-16). Everyone must pass through the troubled times of this age if they hope to reach the next, and the same applies to Israel. About Israel, Uriel agrees with Ezra that the world was created for their sake; nonetheless, he is quick to point out that the sin of Adam has brought about a world-order other than that intended by

God, and has thereby nullified that original intention with regard to Israel. Whereas the next world is worth inheriting, Uriel implies that this present world is not, since it has been transformed by human frailty into a dominion of sin. He concludes, then, by instructing Ezra to adopt an eschatological frame of reference by looking to 'what is to come, rather than what is now present' (7.16).

There is no dispute in studies of 4 Ezra that in episode III Ezra changes from being the spokesperson for Israel to being the spokesperson for humanity trapped in sin. The first indication of this is evident in Ezra's speech in 7.17-18, where Ezra pleads the case not of the righteous but of the wicked, broadening the scope of his concern to encompass the whole of desperate humanity.

Neither should there be any confusion as to how this change in Ezra takes place. It is facilitated by the fact that Ezra recognizes here the import of Uriel's position, which denies to the present age any real concept of God's merciful activity—the very notion that underlay Ezra's three initial appeals to God on the basis that divine mercy is the only solution to Israel's dilemma. Whereas up to this point Ezra's appeals to God have emerged from within a covenantal framework, he now recognizes from Uriel's words that what determines the ways of God is not so much a covenantal relationship with Israel but, more significantly, a temporal distinction between the ages; to speak meaningfully about divine activity, one must be clear about which age is being considered, for on this side of the eschatological boundary such a concept is all but vacuous. The world that resulted from Adam's sin is the kind of world where divine activity is absent. As a consequence, when considering the ways of God in this world, a covenantal framework (dependent as it is on the foundation of God's active mercy in this age) is ancillary to the time-clock of the history of the ages. God cannot be expected to act in this age, although he will certainly enter the theatre of world history at the end of this age.

Ezra has understood the ramifications of Uriel's position, and for this reason, and this reason alone, his occupation shifts from being the ambassador of Israel to being the ambassador of all humanity. Once the covenantal framework is relegated to the periphery of one's perceptions, the nation of Israel stands alongside all other nations before God, and the one who pleaded Israel's case now has a new client in the whole of the human race (a situation already hinted at in Uriel's switch from speaking about Israel in 7.10 to speaking about 'the living' in 7.14). As Ezra has made clear right from the start of episode I, any hope that Israel might have is dependent upon God's salvific initiative, which alone can overcome the Adamic condition of sin in humanity (3.20), and correct the desperate situation facing the people of Israel (3.28-36; 4.22-25; 6.55-59). Without recourse to divine grace, Israel stands alongside the rest of humanity as indistinct from them. The problem, then, is far greater than Ezra had imagined initially, and is not just a question about the absence of God's grace upon Israel in their present situation, but the absence of God's grace altogether from this present age.

So it is that we perceive from this point in episode III a dramatic shift in Ezra's understanding and concerns, since he for the first time has seen the ramifications of Uriel's position. The shift is most noticeable when contrasting his plea on behalf of the wicked among humanity (7.17-18) with his previous speech just verses earlier (6.55-59), where all those beyond the boundaries of Israel were described as 'nothing', 'spittle', as significant as 'a drop from a bucket'. It is precisely those same people, described moments before in strains of degrading polemic, who are now included within Ezra's concerns and pleas.

If the general thrust of Uriel's position has become obvious to Ezra in the way described, there is more to his position, as the continuing dialogue in episode III reveals.

Uriel on the Mechanics of Salvation

Having called into question the notion of divine activity within the present age, Uriel nonetheless demonstrates that God has given humanity all that it needs within the law itself. Proper performance of the law of God is, for Uriel, the solution to the human dilemma, the vehicle that provides transportation from the present age to the next. God has given the law, revealing his expectations concerning 'what they should do to live and what they should observe to avoid punishment' (7.21). The law, however, has been neglected by the wicked who have 'ignored his ways', 'scorned his law', 'denied his covenants', 'been unfaithful to his statutes', and 'not performed his works' (7.23-24). In Uriel's opinion, it is a better thing that the innumerable wicked should perish than that the law of God should be disregarded and invalidated (7.20)—a rather callous attitude that many might find disturbing. As we will see, Ezra is one for whom this is the case.

A comparison of Uriel's case in 7.19-25 (described above) with Ezra's case in 3.4-27 reveals both similarities and differences. In

common, both characters hold that the law is God's way of providing a
way out of a desperate situation, and both hold that the law has
not been well obeyed. In contrast, however, the problem is analysed
differently. For Uriel, the problem is primarily one of human will and
motivation, in that rarely do people live faithfully in accord with God's
law. For Ezra, this analysis is superficial, since the root of the problem
is more fundamental, involving the way in which evil resides within
the human heart. Accordingly, Ezra and Uriel place blame differently
in their respective schemes. Ezra places the blame on God who has
failed to remove the evil heart, thereby making obedience to the law
an unsuccessful enterprise, whereas Uriel places the blame simply on
sinful humanity. For Ezra, blaming humanity for its failure is a peri-
pheral matter, since performance of the law is dependent upon a prior
and more fundamental factor: the initiative of God in providing
merciful assistance. For Uriel, such a factor is ruled out by the
time-frame of the two ages.

Both characters recognize the implications of what Uriel is saying:
that is, very few people can actually hope to be saved. Ezra makes this
clear in 7.45-48. After recognizing that Uriel's position is good news
for the righteous, Ezra despairs of the paltry number of those who
might be seen as righteous because of the evil heart that leads to death,
a condition that affects not just a few but 'almost all who have been
created' (7.48). Perhaps the problem is even more extreme, for, he
says, 'who among the living is there that has not sinned, or who is
there among mortals that has not transgressed your covenant' (7.46).

This situation is not problematic for Uriel, however. After giving
examples of how what is rare is precious while what is common is not
(7.49-59), Uriel states that there will be great rejoicing over the few
who will be saved since they are a precious commodity, but no grief
will be spared for the vast majority who will perish since they are
common and inconsequential.

Their insignificance before God is described in ways similar to Ezra's
earlier views about the insignificance of the gentiles, who are as
conspicuous to God as a drop from a bucket (6.56-57). According to
Uriel, however, it is not the gentiles per se but the vast perishing
multitude who are worthless, as conspicuous to God as a fleeting mist
(7.61). Ezra's earlier views, supported by a traditional covenantal
framework, have been eroded by Uriel's perspective, which now places
not just the gentiles but nearly all humanity in the position Ezra had
thought was held by the gentiles alone. Ezra's ethnic distinction, based

on the presupposition of divine favour towards Israel, has been displaced by a distinction between the many and the few, the former encompassing almost all of humanity and the latter encompassing a minuscule number who are presumably from among the people of Israel but who are hardly exhaustive of Israel's ranks. So it is that Uriel's meaning in 5.40 ('You cannot discover my judgement, or the goal of the love that I have promised to my people') is similar to that in 7.60 ('So also will be the judgement that I have promised'); if the earlier passage could be interpreted as encouragement and assurance to the people of Israel, it is obvious from the later passage that such an understanding of Uriel's position would be a premature and ill-founded judgement, since he now elaborates that the goal of God's eschatological promises will favour only 'the few who shall be saved' (albeit from among the ranks of Israel), rather than the ethnic people of Israel as a whole.

For the most part, the rest of episode III does not advance Uriel's position much but reinforces it, as the dispute between him and Ezra continues. He remains firm in his conviction that transgressors of the law will be condemned to torment and destruction (e.g., 7.37-38, 72-73, 79-80, 81, 130-31; 8.55-58; 9.11-12), a view that was shared by most traditional forms of Judaism but which for Uriel has a radically different meaning, since for him transgressors have little recourse to divine grace to offset their condition. Accordingly, Uriel is unfailing in his belief that the number of those who will be saved is tiny, and he feels no regret over the exceedingly large multitude of humanity who will be destroyed (e.g., 7.131; 8.2-3, 37-41; 9.21-22). The responsibility for this annihilation of most of humanity rests solely on the shoulders of those who will be destroyed, since they have been given the choice either to follow or to abandon God's law (e.g., 7.72, 127-31; 8.55-56; 9.11). Ezra's repeated appeals to divine mercy are ruled out at every turn (see below), since the destiny of everyone is determined by each one's works and performance of the law. So it is that Ezra himself can be numbered among the very few, since he has 'a treasure of works stored up with the Most High' (7.77), just as salvation will be granted to the individual 'on account of their works or on account of the faith in which they have believed [or better: 'on account of their faithfulness in which they have put their trust']' (9.7). That this involves extreme rigour and stringent discipline on the part of the individual is made clear in 7.88-93:

> During the time that they [the righteous] lived in it [the mortal
> body], they laboriously served the Most High, and withstood danger
> every hour, that they might keep the law of the Lawgiver
> perfectly...They have striven with great effort to overcome the evil
> thought [or: the natural impulse towards evil] that was formed with
> them, so that it might not lead them astray from life into death.
> (7.89, 92)

Such sentiments, which put the responsibility for overcoming the
evil heart within the abilities of the individual without recourse to
divine assistance (contrast Ezra's view in 3.20-27), are to be expected if
divine grace and mercy are not to be expected within this present age,
as Uriel has consistently suggested. It is worth recalling the words
of the Qumran hymnist who gives voice to a critical and cardinal
conviction of most pious Jews of that time:

> Righteousness, I know, is not of man, nor is perfection of way of the
> son of man; to the Most High God belong all righteous deeds. The
> way of man is not established except by the Spirit which God
> created for him to make perfect a way for the children of men.
> (1QH 7.29-32)

The contrast with Uriel's perspective reveals just how far Uriel has
taken us from traditional patterns of Jewish thought and piety.

It is worth noting in some detail Uriel's final speech in episode III,
where he recapitulates his views (9.17-23). Although God intended
good things to come from his creation, the ways of humanity
have corrupted this world (9.17-20), and the multitude will perish
accordingly (9.22). Nonetheless, some can expect to enjoy God's
salvation, and these are identified as 'one grape out of a cluster' or,
changing the imagery, as 'one plant out of a great forest' (9.21).

This is significant symbolism, especially in view of the way in which
the symbols of the vine and the grape cluster functioned within the
Judaism of the author's day as vital and potent symbols of the nation of
Israel. As Ezra began his initial speech in episode II, for example, he
compared Israel to the vine selected from all of the trees in the forest
(5.23). Various other Jewish texts of the author's time make the same
identification (compare especially its use in Ps. Philo 12.8-9; 18.10-11;
23.12-13; 28.4; 30.4; 39.7). The symbol of the vine or grape cluster as
representing the nation of Israel is found embossed on Jewish coins of
the Roman period, a time of foreign domination and rising Jewish
nationalism. So too we hear from the Jewish historian Josephus and the
Jewish Mishnah of the golden vines that stood above the golden gate

into the sanctuary of the Herodian temple and made use of the same symbolism of the vine and the grape cluster (*War* 5.210-11; *Antiquities* 15.395; *m. Mid.* 3.8). Evidently, then, these popular symbols functioned to reinforce the strong sense of the election of Israel, held by most pious Jews of the day.

With this background in view, Uriel's depiction of those who will be saved as 'one grape out of a cluster' is dramatic, cutting right through the traditional symbolism and reworking the image to conform to his own understanding. His recasting of the traditional imagery in these diminutive terms is not accidental but reveals clearly what his underlying purpose has been throughout: to redefine traditional concepts and expectations, and to infuse them with new content. This is the case, for instance, with the term 'Israel' itself, which for Ezra designates a distinctive ethnic group, but for Uriel comes to have little ethnic reference; if it is meaningful at all for Uriel, it is as a reference to the few (no doubt, Jews) who earn their way into the next age through their faultless obedience to the law. Another example is the characters' use of the term 'patience'. For Ezra, this characteristic is part and parcel of God's merciful dealings with humanity (cf. 7.134); for Uriel, however, it holds precisely the opposite meaning, reinforcing his two-age scheme and depicting God as one who waits until the next age before acting (7.74).

The same is true for Uriel's description of God's activity in 9.21-22, where God is said to spare some people 'with great difficulty' and to 'perfect' them 'with much labour'. Here it is God who has worked hard for the salvation of the righteous. We should not think, however, that Uriel has surrendered his earlier conviction that salvation is granted to those who perfectly served God by means of their great effort in order to overcome evil (7.89, 92). Uriel has not suddenly changed his tone to affirm that salvation will be granted on the basis of divine grace. He seems instead to be wrapping his position in language that affirms God's sovereignty and justice. This is not wholly unjustifiable on his part for, as the three visions in episodes IV to VI reveal, God will show himself to be the mighty one who defeats the evil that permeates his world and the great deliverer of those who are worthy of salvation. Nonetheless, whatever effort God may be said to expend is not 'grace' in its traditional sense. God will 'save' some, no doubt, in the remarkable eschatological events towards the end of this age, but this is a far cry from what Ezra expects of the God who has the reputation of actively bestowing his grace in the present upon those who seek him.

For Uriel, God's efforts will be operative in the end of the present age, but this benefits only those who have managed to escape an otherwise impossible situation despite preposterous odds.

Ezra on the Mechanics of Salvation

Throughout episode III, Ezra's speeches are just as unbending as Uriel's, marked as they are by the central conviction that the scenario described by Uriel is desperate for almost all humanity unless God takes the initiative to act in ways consonant with his reputation as one full of compassion and mercy. As we have seen (pp. 45-48 above), a first appeal on behalf of Israel (6.38-59) gives way to two further appeals (7.17-18, 45-48), this time on behalf of 'almost all who have been created' (7.48).

On two other occasions, Ezra's agitation provokes profound laments on behalf of humanity. So he cries out:

> Let the human race lament...For all who have been born are entangled in iniquities, and are full of sins and burdened with transgressions. (7.65, 68)

Israel as a part of humanity is nowhere in view. This, of course, is due to the fact that a catastrophic condition encompasses the whole of the human race, erasing national distinctions unless the nation has recourse to a God who chooses to act on its behalf—a situation that Uriel has ruled out in the present period of the progress of the ages. Accordingly, says Ezra, the predicament is pathetic for two reasons: (1) because humanity knows of its pitiful condition (7.62-67), and (2) because no one within the race of humanity is capable of correcting that condition (7.68-69).

A similar lament is evident in 7.116-26, where Ezra charges that it would have been better for the multitude of sinners never to have been born than to live with the torment of knowing that they will have no part in the great glories that will be granted to the few.

After each of these lamentations, Ezra suggests ways in which the situation might be avoided, appealing in the first instance to the hope that those who are righteous might be able to intercede on behalf of sinners, and in the second instance to the hope that God himself will simply intervene on behalf of sinners. The former case (the righteous interceding for the sinners) is concerned with the final day of judgement (7.102-103) and is directly related to Uriel's eschatological descriptions in 7.78-101. Uriel states categorically, however, that the righteous will not be able to intercede for the unrighteous on the day of judgement, since all will be responsible for their own actions (7.104-105). Ezra cannot reconcile this with what he knows of God's ways in the past, as the scriptures illustrate, when God allowed righteous men (Abraham, Moses, Joshua, Samuel, David, Solomon, Elijah, Hezekiah, 'and many others') to make intercession profitably for the ungodly (7.106-111). Uriel, however, does not allow Ezra to abstract principles from the past and expect them to apply in the future (7.112); no mercy will be shown to sinners in the next age.

After his second lament for humanity, and throughout the rest of episode III, Ezra is single-minded in appealing to God to act mercifully in the present on behalf of the wicked, for their only hope lies with his initiating grace. Appeals of this nature are found in three speeches (7.132-40; 8.4-36, 42-45), so important are they to him. In them, Ezra seems to employ any argument that might have some effect. His desperation is apparent, and his various arguments are some of his most interesting and engaging.

The first appeal to God's mercy consists of an extensive recounting of some of the attributes of God, depicting him to be concerned for and involved with humanity (7.132-40). This moving appeal sets up a profound disparity: humanity faces virtual extinction while God advertises himself as the loving and merciful sovereign. If God were uninvolved in the processes of history, the result would be that 'not one ten-thousandth of humanity could have life' (7.139), and 'there would probably be left only very few of the innumerable multitude' (7.140). Here too, Ezra shows that he realizes that the logical conclusion of Uriel's position is the salvation of only a very few. Unsatisfied with Uriel's lack of concern for the perishing, Ezra counters Uriel's case with a portrait of God drawn from the pages of scripture, in which he highlights the following attributes: mercy, graciousness, patience, bounty, and compassion. Even the concept of God's justice is contained within these categories, since God in his goodness is said to relieve sinners of their iniquities (7.138) and pardons those whom he has created, blotting out their multitude of sins (7.139). For Ezra, sinfulness does not disqualify one from God's attention, but actually necessitates it; the sinfulness of humanity should not negate God's favour, but requires it. As we have seen, Uriel agrees with none of this, and his brief rebuttal of 8.1-3 reinforces all that he has already said which runs counter to Ezra's depiction of a merciful God.

Before proceeding to Ezra's second appeal for mercy, it is worth noticing briefly that Ezra's first appeal appears to be indebted to Exodus 34.6-7a:

> The Lord, the Lord, a God merciful and gracious, slow to anger, and abounding in love and steadfastness, keeping steadfast love for thousands, forgiving iniquity, transgression and sin.

This kind of recital of God's character is common stock within Jewish scripture and literature (Neh. 9.17; Pss. 86.15; 103.8-18; 145.8-9; Joel 2.13; Jon. 4.2; Sir. 2.11; Pr. Man. 7; Test. Zeb. 9.7; Wisd. Sol. 15.1), and shares many features of the penitential liturgies of traditional Judaism. Ezra's recital, then, flows naturally from his acquaintance with scripture and his worship of the God who is revealed therein.

This is significant since, just prior to this, Uriel has appealed to scripture in support of his own case (7.129-30). Throughout, Uriel has consistently urged Ezra to look to the events of the future to understand the ways of God properly; the interpretation and application of scripture in answer to Ezra has not entered into Uriel's presentation or defence. In this one instance, however, the message of Moses and the prophets is claimed as the precedent to Uriel's own, as Uriel cites Deuteronomy 30.19 in support of his case.

It is best to understand Ezra's second appeal for divine mercy as consisting of three distinct but interrelated parts. In this lengthy speech, Ezra makes an initial appeal to God to have mercy on humanity (8.4-14), moves to a request for God to save his people (8.15-33), and finally returns to an appeal for the sake of humanity (8.34-36). It will be important to recognize how these three parts cohere.

Appealing on behalf of humanity (8.4-14), Ezra recounts the stages of human development from conception to death in a touching description of the way in which God sustains the whole process and nurtures the individual throughout it all. God, who is shown to be present at every point, is described as the one who alone exists (8.7), a statement that serves either to reinforce Jewish monotheism, highlighting how creation is dependent upon its sole creator, or to place the existence of creation within the very being of its creator (a form of panentheism, 'all within God'). In either case, the result is the same: Ezra sees no sense in God's efforts throughout the entire process of human development if the end result is the destruction of humanity, with salvation going to only a few, as Uriel has just pronounced in 8.1-3. Where is the meaning in God's ways?

Ezra is content, he says, to leave this matter to God, intending now to turn his analysis away from the situation affecting humanity in general to that affecting Israel in particular (8.15-19), describing them as 'your people, for whom I am grieved', 'your inheritance, for whom I lament', 'Israel, for whom I am sad', 'the seed of Jacob, for whom I am troubled'. Ezra here returns to the kind of nationalistic frame of mind that has not been evident in his concerns since his initial speech of episode III (6.55-59).

This nationalistic appeal works in two ways. First, Ezra pleads with God not to look upon the sinners of the nation, but to be merciful by allowing the righteousness of the few within Israel to benefit the whole people (8.26-30). This line of argument is abandoned, however, in 8.31-33 where, changing the nature of his logic, Ezra appeals directly to the mercy of God without mention of the merit of the few, requesting simply that God ignore the sin of Israel. Ezra here presumes that 'works of righteousness' have salvific import only for the righteous few who have many works laid up in heaven and who will receive their reward because of their deeds (8.33). The hope of sinners rests not in the righteous deeds of others being applied to them, but solely in the mercy of God himself (8.31-32). So, then, although Ezra's logic in 8.26-30 and 8.31-33 may run along different lines, the constant in them both is the call upon God to be merciful to Israel.

The first two sections of Ezra's second appeal may appear to be somewhat unrelated—the first pleading humanity's case (8.4-14) and the second pleading Israel's case (8.15-33). In fact, however, it is better to understand their relationship in the light of the Jewish rhetorical technique of a *qal wahomer* argument that moves from a lesser to a greater case: if A is the case, how much more is B the case. Accordingly, Ezra's speech works like this: if God is responsible for the salvation of humanity (8.4-14), how much more is he responsible for the salvation of Israel (8.15-33). Despite all that Ezra has learned from Uriel concerning the divine attitude towards sinners, Ezra considers this kind of rhetorical argument to be strong, even suggesting two ways in which God might save sinners within Israel: (1) by his mercy he might allow the merits of the righteous to benefit the rest (8.26-30), or (2) by his mercy, he might simply pity the sinners for their own sake, despite their lack of works of righteousness (8.31-33).

In 8.34-36, however, Ezra seems to push his plea for Israel into the service of yet another plea for humanity. (So, compare 8.35 with Ezra's speeches for humanity in 7.45-48, 62-69; compare too 8.36 with Ezra's appeal for mercy upon humanity in 7.134, 138-40.) Here Ezra's point is simple, and is based on another *qal wahomer* argument: if God should be merciful to the unrighteous within Israel (as in 8.31-33), how much more should he be merciful to all sinners, regardless of ethnic status (8.34-36). Thus, whereas Ezra gave the impression early on that he would leave aside his appeals on behalf of humanity (8.15), he has in fact constructed throughout 8.20-36 a case which, by means of two arguments 'from the lesser to the greater' (*qal wahomer*), culminates precisely in its appeal for divine mercy upon humanity.

So it is that the whole of Ezra's appeal in 8.4-36, although marked by noticeable shifts in logic, works towards his plea for God's mercy upon all sinners in 8.34-36; Ezra's nationalistic focus of 8.15-33 serves his universal interest, as again we see that the defender of Israel has become the defender of the human race. Israel is still a part of the picture, and holds a unique place in Ezra's concern, but the human condition has taken centre stage in his prosecution against God. If his arguments shift on occasion, the conviction that underlies them has not shifted: God should be merciful to sinners, for that is his reputation and in that reputation lies hope.

Ezra's third appeal to God's mercy in 8.42-45 is much less elaborate than the second, and follows on from Uriel's rejection of the second appeal (8.37-40). Uriel provides an agricultural parable to make his point, in which many seeds may be sown upon the ground, but only a few will take root and grow (8.41). For two reasons, however, Ezra finds this to be a faulty analogy for Uriel's case, and one that actually supports his own case instead. First, seed is dependent upon the proper amount of rainfall, something that is completely out of the control of the seed and lies firmly in God's hands alone (8.43). The implication of this is that creation needs its creator in order to survive, which is just what Ezra has been saying all along. Second, Ezra does not think that seed can be compared to humanity, since God created the latter in his own image, demonstrating how special it is to him (8.44-45). Here again a qal wahomer argument is evident: if God nourishes seed, how much more will he save humanity. Ezra does not miss the chance to put in a good word for Israel at this point (8.45 suggests that if God has mercy on his creation, then he can have mercy on his people), but the focus of his attention is on God in his role as creator. Both of Ezra's points have sprung from the conviction that the creature is wholly dependent upon the creator and is not able to sustain itself. Since it is pointless to make an appeal to the righteous God on the basis of human righteousness, Ezra here appeals to the creator God on the basis of human creatureliness.

Throughout all his appeals, Ezra has presumed a relationship of solidarity between the creator and his creation, and has concentrated his attention on the need for God to act within the sphere of human history and to be merciful to sinners. Ezra's understanding of God and of his salvation has been shaped by the Jewish scriptures, tradition and worship, all of which depict a gracious God who is eager to pardon sinners for the transgressions they have committed (e.g., 7.134, 138-39). Uriel has repeatedly undermined such expectations of God, but for Ezra they are the sole foundation of the hope for salvation.

Once God's active mercy is ruled out of the equation in this age, as Uriel has done, the consequences are clear. First, the desperate situation facing Israel, whose corporate self-identity is based on an awareness of having been chosen by God's grace, begins to pale in view of the more fundamental situation facing the whole of humanity—a shift that is evident in Ezra's perspective in episode III. Second, the basis of salvation shifts from an emphasis on divine mercy to an emphasis on the merits and accomplishments of the individual in faithfully keeping the law, just as Uriel has suggested and as Ezra recognizes (e.g., 8.32-33, 36). Third, following on from the first two points, the fate of humanity is desperately hopeless, since the number of people who have escaped the clutches of sin can only be a tiny few, if any at all. This scenario is unacceptable to Ezra, since it runs contrary both to what the 'mind' can discern about God (e.g., 7.62-69; 8.24-26) and to what can be known about God from scripture and worship (e.g., 7.132-40). Even up to the very end of this long episode, Ezra refuses to give way on this central matter, almost stamping his feet in emphasis as he concludes in protest against the situation described by Uriel (9.14-15). He remains unconvinced to the end, since he cannot reconcile Uriel's position with his own understanding of the merciful God whom he worships.

Further Reading

Some studies on the dialogues

P.G.R. de Villiers, 'Understanding the Way of God: Form, Function and Message of the Historical Review in 4 Ezra 3.4-27', in K.H. Richards (ed.), *SBL Seminar Papers 1981* (Chico, CA: Scholars Press, 1981), pp. 357-78. Ezra's first speech is used as a springboard into the author's general view that God is not active in this world, that history does not reveal him; only a pre-ordained periodization of the ages explains the ways of God, offering hope through the vision of another world to come.

M.E. Stone, 'The Way of the Most High and the Injustice of God in 4 Ezra', in R. van den Broek *et al.* (eds.), *Knowledge of God in the Graeco-Roman World* (Leiden: Brill, 1988), pp. 132-42; now appears in Stone's *Selected Studies in Pseudepigrapha and Apocrypha* (Leiden: Brill, 1991), pp. 348-58. Explores Ezra's passionate desire to understand the ways of God within the historical realm, despite his present circumstances.

B.W. Longenecker, *Eschatology and the Covenant*, pp. 50-98. Each episode is analysed independently, noting the theological dynamics of the unfolding dialogues. A more extensive reading of the dialogues than is offered in this guide.

J.C.H. Lebram, 'The Piety of the Jewish Apocalyptists', in D. Hellholm (ed.), *Apocalypticism in the Mediterranean World and the Near East* (Tübingen: Mohr [Paul Siebeck], 1983), pp. 171-210, esp. 199-207. Analyses aspects of Ezra's religious problems, the law in its ironic position of being the solution which is unattainable, and the hope held out for Israel as the vessel of the law in this age.

J.R. Levison, *Portraits of Adam in Early Judaism* (JSPSup 1; Sheffield: JSOT Press, 1988), pp. 113-27. A description of the role of Adam within the dialogues.

M.C. de Boer, *The Defeat of Death* (JSNTSup 22; Sheffield: JSOT Press), pp. 73-78. An analysis of the significance of the Adam-sin-death triumvirate in the dialogues.

A.L. Thompson, *Responsibility for Evil in the Theodicy of IV Ezra*, pp. 157-218. A detailed description of the content and character of the dialogues, often very helpful, although the author often poses questions owing more to his own agenda than to that of the text itself.

W. Mundle, 'Das religiöse Problem des IV. Esrabuches', *ZAW* 47 (1929), pp. 222-49. Despite its date, this article is valuable in demonstrating theological issues under consideration in 4 Ezra.

W. Harnisch, 'Der Prophet als Widerpart und Zeuge der Offenbarung: Erwägungen zur Interdependenz von Form und Sache im IV. Buch Esra', in D. Hellholm (ed.), *Apocalypticism in the Mediterranean World and the Near East* (Tübingen: Mohr [Paul Siebeck], 1983), pp. 461-93, esp. 472-78. An analysis of the unfolding drama between Ezra and Uriel, with Ezra representing the voice of a heretical scepticism that is countered at every point by the angel, whose position is ultimately affirmed by Ezra.

U. Luck, 'Das Weltverständnis in der jüdischen Apokalyptik dargestellt am äthiopischen Henoch und am 4. Esra', *ZTK* 73 (1976), pp. 283-305. In an apocalyptic worldview, understanding is not gained from everyday experience and scripture, but only through divine revelation, either of the heavenly realm that reveals a unified world under divine control (1 Enoch), or of a future world where righteousness is established (4 Ezra).

K. Koch, 'Esras erste Vision: Weltzeiten und Weg des Höchsten', *BZ* 22 (1978), pp. 46-75. The positions of the two characters are analysed for their different understandings of the ways of God within this world.

5

EZRA'S TRANSFORMATION
EPISODE IV

Matters of Continuity and Development in Episode IV

Getting through the first three episodes is not easy work because of the length of those episodes and the frustration that arises from them in relation to the dynamics of the dialogues. The reader may be discouraged, then, to find the fourth episode beginning in much the same way as the first three: Ezra's heart is 'troubled again as it was before' (9.27), and this results in his speaking to the Most High (9.28). All this we have seen in the first three episodes, and the reader may think that we are in store for another long and disagreeable dispute.

There are, however, significant indicators to counter this impression. First, there is the command given to Ezra at the end of episode III not to fast any longer (9.23), which runs contrary to Uriel's commands in earlier episodes (5.13, 20; 6.31, 35). Now Ezra is commanded to eat the flowers of the field, which he does (9.24, 26), and from them he finds nourishment and satisfaction (9.26). These symbols of deprivation (fasting) and nourishment (eating) are important structural indicators, signalling that the events of this episode will take on a different character from those of the previous episodes. The same is reinforced by a second indicator: the change of location from Ezra's room where the first three episodes had taken place (3.1) to an open field 'where no house has been built' (9.24, 26), from lying on his bed (3.1) to lying on the grass (9.27).

These changes in diet and location raise the expectation that something different is about to happen in this episode, despite the fact that Ezra's heart is still troubled. As the episode unfolds, these expectations will be fulfilled, as a new Ezra emerges and dialogues give way to revelatory apocalyptic visions. As such, this episode shares some of the characteristics of the preceding dialogues and some of the characteristics of the vision episodes that follow it.

If we see something of a transformed Ezra in this episode, it is not wholly clear where the transformation is first evident. Scholars are divided on the matter. For some, Ezra's 'conversion' is only evident halfway through episode IV (beginning at 10.5), while for others it is noticeable already in his opening speech of episode IV (9.29-37). The issue is whether Ezra's words in 9.26-37 are a complaint (in the same vein as his previous complaints), followed by an event that transforms him (9.38–10.24), or whether the first appearance of a transformed Ezra is evident already in 9.26-37, this transformation being illustrated further in the events of 9.38–10.24. There is no dispute, however, that the encounter between Ezra and the woman (9.38–10.24) clearly reveals a new aspect in Ezra's character, as demonstrated below.

Indications of Change in 9.38-10.24

After Ezra's initial speech, there suddenly appears on stage a woman who is mourning for her deceased son. The woman tells Ezra how she had been barren until she sought out the assistance of God, who pitied her condition and gave her a son. In return she gave glory to God. On the day of her son's wedding, however, he died, and now she mourns for him and longs to die herself (9.38–10.4).

Although the woman in this episode will later be transformed into a heavenly city (10.25-27) and will play a symbolic role in Uriel's interpretation (10.38-55), at this point she functions in a different role. In the descriptions of the mourning woman, there is a striking resemblance between her condition and that of Ezra in episodes I to III: she is 'mourning and weeping with a loud voice', 'deeply grieved at heart' (9.38), 'embittered in spirit and deeply afflicted' (9.41); although she previously sought out God and gave him great glory for his graciousness (9.44-45), she now refuses to be consoled; although others had tried to soothe her troubled heart (10.2-3), she would not be comforted; instead, she intends to 'neither eat nor drink, but without ceasing mourn and fast until I die' (10.4).

So Ezra, too, has repeatedly announced the fact of his troubled heart (3.1; 5.34; 6.36; 9.27), his distress (6.37), his agitation (3.3) and his grief (5.21, 34). In the light of the destruction of Jerusalem and God's apparent betrayal of his people, Ezra, like the woman, could give no glory to God and found no comfort or consolation in Uriel's explanations of God's ways. Just as the woman now fasts, so too did Ezra in the first three episodes. Although the woman is fasting since she would prefer to die, her fast symbolizes her single-mindedness with regard to the issue which torments her. Without relief from her troubles, there is no reason to carry on with life (10.4, 18). This sounds much like Ezra's great lament over humanity in 7.116-126, where the point is made repeatedly: What good is it to live? The same sentiments are voiced by Ezra in 4.12 and 5.35, which, with a few substitutions of terms, could easily have been recited by the woman in her initial condition depicted in episode IV.

If the woman embodies the kind of attitudes and behaviour evidenced by Ezra in episodes I to III, Ezra here does not join her in her disgruntlement but now takes the place held by Uriel in the earlier episodes. In his reply to the woman, Ezra makes two long speeches of rebuke, both of which culminate in similar kinds of advice: keep sorrow in check, put sadness aside, bear adversity bravely, and acknowledge that God is just (10.15-16, 24). This will put her on the road to recovery for, if she does as Ezra instructs, she will find the consolation that eludes her, 'a relief from your troubles' (10.24). Ezra's words in 10.16 imply that the woman's troubled heart had undermined her confidence in God's justice, a situation reminiscent of Ezra's own in the first three episodes. Uriel has already implied that a recognition of God's justice will result in relief from distress (e.g., 5.56–6.6; 6.25-28, 33-34; 7.15-16); Ezra seems simply to have borrowed this point in his assurances to the woman.

The parallel between Ezra and Uriel is seen in other minor features of 9.38–10.24, but here only one of the most notable aspects of Ezra's transformation will be noted, evident in his words of 10.10: 'almost all go to perdition, and a multitude of them will come to doom'. This is an accurate articulation of the view espoused by Uriel in episode III and against which Ezra had reacted so strongly throughout most of that long episode. His dissatisfaction with this view of the salvation of the few is evident even in his closing words of complaint in that episode (9.14-16). The Ezra of 9.38–10.24, however, has evidently resigned himself to accept that, despite the tragedy of this scenario (10.9-15), it should not undermine one's confidence in God nor result in complaint against God (10.15-16), for he is just (10.16). The transformation of Ezra has taken on striking proportions.

These and other factors demonstrate that the woman who appears in episode IV assumes the position held earlier by Ezra, Ezra himself now taking the place held earlier by Uriel. The mourning woman and the tutoring Ezra of episode IV parody the mourning Ezra and the tutoring Uriel of episodes I to III. Gone is any sense of Ezra's complaining, indicting spirit, and there is no sense of an inner struggle in affirming what he previously could not bring himself to accept. He has accepted it simply because it must be accepted, as he says to the women: 'Let yourself be persuaded' (10.20). All this captures in narrative form the fact that Ezra has undergone a transformation in his understanding of and confidence in God, a transformation facilitated by a prior change of heart.

Indicators of Change in Ezra's Initial Speech of Episode IV

If a marked change is evident in the Ezra of 9.38–10.24, is it apparent there for the first time or might it also be noticeable in 9.26-37? Many take the view that Ezra is depicted in 9.26-37 in the same terms as those of the first three episodes, and that his transformation takes place only as he encounters the woman. In favour of this is the fact that Ezra is troubled as the episode begins (9.27), as in all of the earlier episodes, and that after the appearance of the woman Ezra speaks in 9.39 and 10.5 of putting aside the matters that he had been considering. Ezra's initial speech of this episode, then, is thought to be a complaint to God as all the others had been, a complaint interrupted by the appearance of a woman with whom Ezra converses. The conversion of Ezra's demeanour takes place only after he encounters the woman who, in psychological terms, is an externalized projection of Ezra's inner destructive grief and complaint (indicated by his abandoning of his troubled thoughts in 9.39 and 10.5), thereby allowing him to internalize a healthy new spiritual condition marked out by confidence in the justice of God.

It may be, however, that we can find traces of Ezra's transformation already in his speech of 9.29-37. Ezra begins this episode by recounting how God had appeared to Israel's forefathers and had given his law to Israel in order to glorify them. This historical review in 9.29-31 parallels the historical review of his first speech in 3.16-19, their similarities being so apparent that the two could easily be interchanged without interrupting the flow of Ezra's words on either occasion. Perhaps, then, we are to think that Ezra is back where he began, that nothing which transpired in the first three episodes had any effect upon him, that episode IV is to be yet another sustained dispute between two ill-matched rhetoricians. But this perception is muted as Ezra continues in 9.32-37, where Ezra's attitude towards the people's failure to observe the law is evident. In 3.20-27 the people's failure was shown to have frustrated the salvific potential of the law, just as in Ezra's words here, but now a new attitude is apparent in Ezra's analysis. Whereas Ezra had argued in 3.20-36 that God was to be blamed for the people's failure to keep the law, in 9.32-37 nothing of the sort is evident. In episode IV, in contrast to the first episode, the blame for the people's failure is wholly their own and is due to their disobedience. The responsibility falls directly upon them rather than upon God; complaints against God are nowhere in sight in any of this.

This impression receives some reinforcement in Ezra's illustration in 9.34-37, which draws out a general principle learned from nature and experience of life: a container is not spoiled when its contents spoil, demonstrating that the container is more significant than that which it contains. Applied to the people and the law, this should mean that the people of Israel (who 'contain' the law) are greater than the law. Ezra notes that the rule does not apply in this case, however. Since Ezra's tone of voice is not audible to the reader, it is possible to hear this as another indictment against God, indicating that God has broken a general rule, to Israel's detriment, demonstrating that Ezra's transformation has yet to occur. If this were the case, however, it would be a very subtle charge against God, and Ezra's initial complaints have never been subtle. His habit has always been to confront God directly and charge him explicitly, calling on him to account for his ways. Nothing of the sort appears here, suggesting that this is not a vague indictment of God. Instead, Ezra's point is that the principle that is drawn from nature and from experience cannot be applied to the people and the law, since God's law does not conform to the general categories of life (9.31-32) and since the law, unlike the people themselves, is imperishable and glorious (9.32, 37).

This speech, then, has close parallels with Uriel's views expressed in the earlier dialogues. First, Uriel has been quick to point out that God's ways transcend the limits of human reckoning (4.1-21; 5.31-40), just as Ezra now invalidates the drawing of principles from human experience and applying them to God and God's law. Second, throughout the earlier episodes Ezra pleaded on behalf of Israel and humanity, and nowhere was he prepared to affirm the honour of the law at their expense. Here, however, he does precisely that. This is reminiscent of

Uriel's point all along, as is most evident in his words of 7.20: 'Let the many perish who are now living, rather than that the law of God which is set before them be disregarded'. Ezra's illustration in 9.34-37, then, does not constitute a subtle complaint against God, but affirms that the ways of God are just. God is not implicated, nor is there an appeal to divine mercy on behalf of Israel. Although the scenario of Israel's fate is troubling to Ezra, he nonetheless accepts that all is as it should be and that God is above reproach since the people themselves are to blame.

This is certainly significant. The pattern in episodes I to III has established that, whenever Ezra initiates a new dialogue, he begins with an appeal to God on behalf of Israel. In episode IV, however, no such appeal appears. Instead, Ezra simply reflects on the situation without appeal to a solution or an explanation from God. Ezra describes a scenario in which those who do not keep the law will perish, and he has no expectation that this should be changed. Evidently, then, during the seven-day interval between episodes III and IV, Ezra has resigned himself (off-stage) to Uriel's general point of view. Ezra is still troubled, but appears to have accepted that the situation is as Uriel described it. At the conclusion of episode III, Ezra was unconvinced by Uriel's position. Ezra's perspective may have broadened in episode III to include a universal focus, but his line of argument remained consistent throughout: it is only by God's active grace that anyone can hope for salvation. Here in episode IV, however, Ezra does not plead for God's mercy, as he had before, nor does he argue, as he had previously, that the honour of Israel's forefathers or the giving of the law should enable Israel to have special consideration. Not only are Ezra's words in his initial speech of episode IV unlike his words in episodes I to III, they could easily have been expressed by Uriel at many places throughout the previous dialogues. Ezra's words in 9.36-37 are almost identical to those of Uriel in 7.20, and his speech parallels Uriel's speeches in 7.20-25, 70-74 and 127-31.

Ezra's Affirmation of God's Justice, Despite his own Sorrow

If Ezra has adopted a new attitude in episode IV, it is not depicted as a callous attitude, for the encounter between Ezra and the mourning woman introduces an important distinction between proper and improper modes of mourning and grief. Before his initial speech in episode IV, Ezra admits his troubled heart, but he goes on to affirm in

9.27-39 that it is proper for sinners to be destroyed because of their disobedience to God's law. Although he is disturbed about this, he does nothing to doubt God's justice in the matter. Similarly, in 10.6-24, where Ezra portrays the woman's loss as insignificant when compared to the greater loss of human destruction, Ezra's sorrow for Israel and for humanity is evident, but he does not allow his remorse to degenerate into an accusation against God as he had in earlier episodes. Ezra's grief is still evident, but he now controls it; he now affirms God's justice and, accordingly, is able to bear his sorrow. In contrast, however, the woman's mourning stifles her ability to affirm that God is just. It is only because her grief has undermined her confidence in God that Ezra rebukes her; there is nothing wrong with mourning itself, as he himself states (9.27; 10.8). In fact, in 10.39 (cf. 10.50), we hear that God looks favourably upon Ezra precisely because he has 'sorrowed continually' for Israel, and 'mourned greatly over Zion'. Grief is acceptable so long as it does not overturn one's confidence in God and certainty of God's righteousness.

This point is important theologically and psychologically, but it also provides us with further evidence for thinking that Ezra's conversion is already evident in 9.27-36. The factors against this view of 9.27-36 are, as noted earlier, (1) Ezra's grief, and (2) the mention in 9.39 and 10.5 of putting aside the thoughts which were occupying him. The first is not a problem, since grief in itself is not an indication of an adverse posture towards God, as we have seen.

Nor is the second problematic. Ezra's statements that he put his grievous thoughts behind him (9.39; 10.5) do not imply that his speech was interrupted by the appearance of the woman before he could make an explicit complaint against God, nor that only with the appearance of the woman in 9.38 does he silence his complaints. Instead, these declarations function in precisely the opposite manner, confirming that Ezra is not prepared to entertain complaints against God. If the reader expects to hear from Ezra's initial speech a complaint concerning God's ways, or an appeal to God's mercy on behalf of Israel, as has been his consistent practice in all of his initial speeches earlier, Ezra puts such expectations aside with his words in 9.39; no appeal to God's intervention and no complaint about God's ways will be entertained by him now. The implication is clear: God's ways are above reproach, for things, as troublesome as they are, are as they should be. Ezra's statement in 9.39 signals that his words to the Most High have ended, and they have ended in ways contrary to the expected precedent, without complaint or appeal. He has spoken his mind in 9.29-37, and there is nothing more to come; sinners perish in order that the law might retain its glory. Despite the fact that this is a troubling prospect, he sees no reason to amend this situation. Ezra's grief remains, but it is properly managed.

The second occurrence of this phrase in 10.5 operates in the same way. After hearing the whole of the woman's case, Ezra stands firm in his resolve that complaints and appeals are inappropriate. Rather than empathizing with the distraught woman, as he might well have done in episodes I to III, Ezra does not waver from his recent acceptance of the justice of God's ways. After hearing her sorrowful story, Ezra fails to petition God on her behalf or to join in with her resentment. Instead, he answers her 'in anger' (10.5), instructing her to affirm God's justice. Once again, then, this verse does nothing to illustrate that Ezra's attitude is changed only after encountering the sorrowful woman. Instead, it demonstrates that the change within Ezra evident already in 9.29-36 is firm, that his newly-acquired confidence in God is impervious to even the most traumatic situations. There is, then, no complaint to follow Ezra's opening speech and, unlike the woman, Ezra has resolved that God's ways are not to be questioned. Again, the trauma of the situation is troublesome, but Ezra does not allow his troubled heart to result in an indictment against God.

At each point of our analysis of episode IV we have come face to face with an Ezra radically transformed from the Ezra of episodes I to III. He still feels troubled by the situation as he describes it, but now his grief is kept in check, and he does not allow it to undermine his confidence in God. The figures of the woman and Ezra embody two forms of grief, improper and proper, unhealthy and healthy. The Ezra of episode IV has accepted the general outline of Uriel's position (9.29-36), has put aside his indictments of God (9.39; 10.5), and now preaches what he had not allowed himself to affirm: that debilitating sorrow should give way to confidence in the justice of God, with the result that one will be consoled (10.15-16, 24). Here the patient has become the doctor, and the medicine he prescribes is that which he himself had earlier refused. According to his own prescription in 10.15-16 and 10.24, because he now affirms that God is just, so he can now expect to be consoled. It is this expectation that triggers the events of the second half of episode IV.

The First Vision of Hope

As soon as Ezra instructs the woman to put aside her unhealthy sorrow, to his amazement her face shone and 'flashed like lightning' (10.25). At this, Ezra became extremely afraid as he failed to understand what had happened. Then the woman gave a 'loud and fearful cry' (10.26) and was transformed into a great city with 'huge foundations' (10.27). Again Ezra is said to be afraid at this, crying out in a loud voice for Uriel who, according to Ezra, 'brought me into this overpowering bewilderment' (10.28). Throughout 10.29-37 Ezra remains in this frame of mind, blaming Uriel for his condition (10.28, 32), begging him not to forsake him (10.34), and asking him for an explanation of all this that he is not able to understand (10.32, 35-37).

This characterization of Ezra is intriguing, and is marked by dramatic irony. He has been proclaiming that, by affirming God's justice, one will find relief from sorrow. Ezra has already affirmed God's justice in this episode; what is still to come, then, is his consolation. Instead of being consoled, however, Ezra sees a vision that he cannot comprehend and that frightens and troubles him more than ever. Despite all his complaints of episodes I to III, Ezra has taken the only option open to him and appropriated in episode IV Uriel's confident understanding of God's just ways, expecting from this to find comfort, rather than further frustration. Now, more bewildered than ever, he feels himself to have been abandoned by Uriel, and so he blames Uriel for his present distress. The irony is in what Ezra fails to realize: that the vision that now troubles him greatly is, in fact, part of the process whereby he finds his consolation. This becomes apparent to him from the interpretation of these disturbing events (10.38-60).

In his role as angelic interpreter of the visions, Uriel is no longer Ezra's dialogical opponent, as in episodes I to III, but now functions as Ezra's ally, lending assistance to Ezra's quest. (This is not surprising, in view of the fact that Ezra now stands in the place held by Uriel in the earlier episodes.) Accordingly, Uriel interprets the vision so that Ezra, who has been in a state of constant sorrow (10.39, 50), can understand and be comforted. It comes as no surprise, then, when Uriel concludes his interpretation with the words, 'Therefore do not be afraid, and do not let your heart be terrified' (10.55). Here Ezra finds his consolation. Having resigned himself to be retrained in his understanding of the ways of God, Ezra finds here the first assurance that he was right to do so.

Not all the details of what Ezra has seen are explained in the interpretation, but the basic point is this: the woman represents the heavenly Jerusalem who is mourning for the destruction of Jerusalem, but who herself remains great and splendid (10.38-59). Ezra is shown the 'brightness of her glory, and the loveliness of her beauty' (10.50), and is commanded to go into the city to see its splendour and vastness (10.55). In the process, Uriel expects Ezra to leave behind his troubled heart.

The primary import of the vision is not to affirm that a new Jerusalem will be built on earth in the future; instead, it functions to reinforce a perspective of God and his ways that is not dependent upon an earthly city. Its purpose is not to establish confidence in the rebuilding of the Judaean city or its temple, but to shift the focus to the heavenly world and the hope for the world to come. So, in Uriel's interpretation, the destruction of the earthly city is noted in 10.48, but this does not result in the assurance of a restored, earthly city; his comments that follow immediately in 10.49-55 are instead focused exclusively on the heavenly city. All this serves to transfer the attention away from the earthly, historical sphere and towards the heavenly, eschatological sphere.

This vision in episode IV is, then, the first confirmation of Uriel's descriptions of the age to come; the heavenly Zion is in existence now and will be revealed to those who are deserving in the age to come. That a glorious Zion has been preserved serves both to give Ezra comfort and hope and to certify that he was right to accept Uriel's understanding and confidence as his own. The two visions that follow in episodes V and VI function in the same fashion and expand further what Ezra has seen in episode IV.

Further Reading

On the importance of episode IV within the progression of the narrative

M.E. Stone, 'Reactions to Destructions of the Second Temple: Theology, Perception and Conversion', *JSJ* 12 (1981), pp. 195-204; now appears in Stone's *Selected Studies in Pseudepigrapha and Apocrypha*, pp. 429-38. A broad study comes to focus on the fourth episode of 4 Ezra as the pivotal episode of the book, depicting the conversion experience of Ezra. The episode reveals the manner in which the author's own anxiety found resolution.

M.E. Stone, 'On Reading an Apocalypse', in J.J. Collins and J.H. Charlesworth (eds.), *Mysteries and Revelations*, pp. 65-78, esp. 73-75. The role reversal of episode IV demonstrates the author's own 'externalization' of pain and 'internalization' of comfort.

A.L. Thompson, *Responsibility for Evil in the Theodicy of IV Ezra*, pp. 218-34. Highlights the transitional nature of episode IV as illustrative of the author's own experience.

E. Breech, 'These Fragments I Have Shored Against my Ruins: The Form and Function of 4 Ezra', *JBL* 92 (1973), pp. 267-74. Demonstrates the role of this episode within the larger purposes of the text, moving from turmoil to consolation.

W. Harnisch, 'Die Ironie Der Offenbarung: Exegetische Erwägungen zur Zionvision im 4. Buch Esra', in K.H. Richards (ed.), *SBL Seminar Papers 1981* (Chico, CA: Scholars Press, 1981), pp. 79-104. A technical study of the form and content of this episode in relation to the theological questions posed by Ezra in the earlier dialogues.

6

THE TRIUMPH OF GOD:
EPISODES V AND VI

Introduction to the Visions

Whereas all the previous episodes begin with an initial speech from
Ezra, episodes V and VI do not follow that pattern, but begin as Ezra
receives a vision. These two visions build on episode IV, providing
further consolidation and affirmation of Ezra's new perspective. This is
not immediately apparent to Ezra, however. So, for instance, after the
vision in episode V, Ezra awakes 'terrified' (12.5) and 'in great per-
plexity of mind and great fear' (12.3b; cf. 12.5). As in episode IV, so
here the vision does not immediately bring about the comfort for
which Ezra had hoped, and so he calls upon God to show him the
'interpretation and meaning of this terrifying vision so that you may
fully comfort my soul' (12.8). The same is true of the vision in episode
VI, where Ezra's fear prompts him to request an explanation of what
he has seen (13.13b-15). Ezra has learned from his experiences in
episode IV that comfort will be granted to him by means of divine
explanation. The import of the mysterious visions V and VI remains
ambiguous until they are interpreted by Uriel.

Although each of these episodes consists of four parts, the episodes
are structurally identical in their first three parts:

1. the vision (eagle in 11.1-12.3a; man from the sea in 13.1-13a)
2. Ezra's plea for an explanation (12.3b-9; 13.13b-20)
3. the interpretation of the vision (12.10-34; 13.21-52)

Many believe that much of the vision and interpretation material in
these two episodes is drawn from established traditions already known
by the author, although his own hand is evident in places, especially in

the interpretation of the vision in episode VI. Although a brief discussion of the fourth part of episode VI (13.53-58) appears at the end of this chapter, discussion of the fourth part of episode V (12.35-51) will appear in the next chapter of this guide.

The vision in episode V is usually referred to as the Eagle Vision, named after the eagle that is shown to rise up from the sea with three heads and twelve wings. This eagle reigns oppressively over the whole earth until a lion appears, roars accusations against the eagle, and announces the end of the age as the eagle is burned up in judgement. This eschatological vision is shot through with political symbolism. The beast is representative of Rome, whose rule covered the world that mattered in the first century CE. The three heads of the beast represent the Roman emperors Vespasian, Titus and Domitian. The lion is obviously the messiah of Israel, later identified as being of the royal line of David (12.32), who overthrows the evil reign of Rome.

In the vision of the Man from the Sea (sometimes referred to as the Son of Man Vision), Ezra sees 'something like the figure of a man' rising up from the sea into the clouds of heaven (13.3). A multitude of men gather to make war against him, but he destroys the multitudes with a stream of fire from his mouth. He then calls to himself another multitude, a peaceable one, while others come to him from far and wide. Here the culprit is not a specific political entity (Rome) but the whole of the nations of the world, who are destroyed by the messiah at the end of the age. The nationalistic character of the tradition shows through the page especially in 13.12-13, in which we are told of the gathering of a peaceable multitude as well as those who come from afar; in all likelihood, the former was originally a reference to the salvation of the Judaean Jewry who enjoy a peaceful existence after the advent of the messiah, while the latter represented the return of the diaspora Jews who also share in the glory of the messianic age in the holy land of Israel.

It is important to notice that the contents of both episodes V and VI are influenced by the apocalyptic vision of Daniel 7. This is true of minor details (e.g. the stirring up of the waves in 4 Ezra 13.2 and Dan. 7.2), and of more significant features as well. So, in the vision of the Man from the Sea in episode VI, the reference to 'something like the figure of a man' in 13.3 seems to be indebted to the mention of 'one like a son of man' in Dan. 7.13. This Danielic influence is mentioned explicitly in the Eagle Vision of episode V (12.11-12), as Uriel explains to Ezra the vision that he had seen:

> The eagle that you saw coming up from the sea is the fourth
> kingdom that appeared in a vision to your brother Daniel. But it was
> not explained to him as I now explain to you.

The fourth kingdom to which Uriel refers is depicted in Dan. 7.7 and
7.23 not as an eagle but as a beast—a cryptic reference to the Greek
empire of the author's day. The physical appearance of the beast in
Daniel diverges drastically from the physical appearance of an eagle in 4
Ezra, and this accords with the author's concern to update the vision of
Daniel with new significance for his own day. His strategy is transparent, since the eagle was the recognized symbol of Rome and its
empire—the culprit in the destruction of Jerusalem for which Ezra has
mourned throughout the book.

Accordingly, although the specifics of the two visions are determined primarily by the events of the late first century CE, the frame of
reference in which those specifics are portrayed is indebted to the
biblical precedent of the Danielic vision of the eschatological triumph
of God. The author of 4 Ezra invites his audience to interpret events of
the present in the light of the ancient biblical story. The author expects
his audience to make an imaginative act of correspondence between
their day and Daniel's, thereby drawing lessons for the present from the
situation of the past. Daniel's eschatological visions offered hope to the
righteous, assuring them that the network of evil that had ensnared
their world and had brought persecution and suffering would be overcome by a mightier power, and that the faithfulness of the righteous
would not go unnoticed by the God who reigns supremely over this
world. The broad strokes of this scriptural account reverberate within
the fifth and sixth episodes of 4 Ezra and help to promote a sense of
hope and confidence in the God of the Daniel narrative. In this way,
the Danielic account offers the author of 4 Ezra a symbolic resource
from which to shape his readers' perceptions of the world and their
place in it.

The Eagle Vision of Episode V

The vision of episode V depicts Rome, in the form of an eagle, in all
of its power and magnificence as the sovereign political entity of Ezra's
world. So, Ezra states in 11.2, 5-6:

> I saw it spread its wings over the whole earth…and it reigned over
> the earth and over those who inhabit it. And I saw how all things
> under heaven were subjected to it, and no one spoke against it—not
> a single creature that was on the earth.

The eagle, in accord with the bizarre imagery of apocalyptic visions, has twelve wings, eight little wings, and three heads. The complicated description of their actions throughout 11.1-35 is likely to be a coded allegory of a political situation easily recognizable to a first-century audience perhaps, but the specific details of the allegory are, for the most part, no longer clear. The little wings may refer to minor political or military figures of whom we know nothing, but the three heads are depicted in ways that seem to allow an identification with three Roman emperors: Vespasian (69-79 CE), Titus (79-81 CE), and Domitian (81-96 CE).

The interpretation given by Uriel of this vision is a also a complicated piece of coded historical referencing, and is no longer completely decipherable. If the interpretation is largely a piece of pre-existing material that the author has borrowed and incorporated, it may be the case that the interpretation itself has been updated on occasion prior to its inclusion in 4 Ezra, thereby allowing the original vision to take on new significance for its various audiences over time, the early elements of the interpretation appearing side by side with the later elements; such reinterpretation of older traditions is frequently to be found in apocalyptic writings. In its present state, the major features of the interpretation are its allusions to the political rule of Rome's successive leaders (12.10-30) and its reference to the messiah of the tribe of David, symbolized by the lion, who destroys the evil reign of Rome (12.31-33) and saves a remnant of God's people (12.34).

It is probably significant that in the vision itself the eagle rises 'from the sea' (11.1). This detail derives from Dan. 7.3, where the four beasts of Daniel's vision come up out of the sea. In much ancient literature, the sea represents the primordial abyss, often thought to be the abode of evil and its instruments. So, for instance, in the Christian Apocalypse of John (a contemporary of 4 Ezra), we hear of the murder of Christian witnesses by a beast who comes up out of the abyss (Rev. 11.7). Later, the dragon (that is, the 'ancient serpent called the devil or Satan, who leads the whole world astray', Rev. 12.9) gives his authority to a beast to rule in this world (again, the reference is to Rome), this beast having come up from the sea (13.1). The same kind of mythological imagery may lie behind the image of the eagle's thalassic origins in 4 Ezra 11.1.

It needs to be noted, however, that the messianic figure of 4 Ezra 13 in episode VI, who is a divine being, is also said to arise out of the sea (13.3). Perhaps, then, in each of these visions the sea serves only as the point of origin for the initial details of the apocalyptic visions, the deep recesses out of which mysterious apocalyptic visions take their shape, without conveying any of the usual mythical connotations associated with it. At any rate, the mythic connotations are absent in the interpretation of the vision in episode VI. When Ezra asks why the divine 'man' came up from the heart of the sea (no doubt emphasizing the last word), the response in 13.51-52 is:

> Just as no one can explore or know what is in the depths of the sea,
> so no one on earth can see my Son or those who are with him,
> except in the time of his day.

Nonetheless, while this interpretation may apply in the later account of the man in episode VI, it is highly likely that the reference to the eagle arising out of the sea in 11.1 was meant to convey all the typical associations of evil normally connected to the imagery.

This view of the Roman empire as the embodiment of evil contrasts sharply with the pro-Roman attitude of the Jewish historian Josephus—a near contemporary of the author of 4 Ezra who a wrote extensive volumes on Jewish history after the destruction of Jerusalem in the late first century CE. Although he had helped (whether willingly or apprehensively; it is difficult to tell) to lead the Jewish revolt against Rome prior to the destruction of Jerusalem in 70 CE, Josephus later recorded the events of the war and depicted Rome as having been the instrument of God in punishing a sinful people (e.g. *War*, 2.390; 5.368-69, 376-8, 412). So too, in the New Testament Paul writes in Romans 13 of the state 'authorities' having been 'established by God'; they are 'God's servants' through whom order is maintained in God's world (13.1-7).

For the authors of 4 Ezra and the Christian Apocalypse of John, however, Rome was the purest manifestation of evil. Despite advertising itself as the keeper of peace, order and security throughout the known world (*pax Romana*), Rome was considered by these two authors to be animated by and permeated with evil, whose point of origin is the sea, the abode of chaotic forces that run contrary to the ways of God. Behind Rome's claims to maintain stability and order, these authors perceive its reign as the means by which chaotic forces of evil are perpetuated throughout the world.

The mighty eagle, then, is depicted as a despotic sovereign (despite the rise and fall of its various little wings), whose rule originates from and is imbibed with evil. Its oppressive reign against all the inhabitants of the earth is recorded (11.32) and used as evidence against it in a powerfully moving indictment of its tyranny and injustice:

> You have held sway over the world with great terror, and over all
> the earth with grievous oppression; and for so long you have lived
> on the earth with deceit. You have judged the earth, but not with
> truth, for you have oppressed the meek and injured the peaceable;
> you have hated those who tell the truth, and have loved liars; you
> have destroyed the homes of those who brought forth fruit, and have
> laid low the walls of those who did you no harm. (11.40-42)

The root of all this is said to have been 'insolence' and 'pride' (11.43).

This is a sober and sombre portrait. The harsh realities stand centre-stage. This world's desperate condition is not glossed over, avoided, or sweetened up; instead, it appears in bold relief, starkly depicted in all its harshness and severity. As in the early episodes of 4 Ezra, so now, this recognition of a world out of joint poses a threat to the sovereignty and justice of God, the creator of this world. But this vision climaxes in a declaration of the sovereignty and power of God, who is soon to bring in his reign of justice. This is the message of the mighty lion, who speaks against the eagle. God has not been blind to all that has been happening in this world, nor is he unable to exercise control; he has seen all, and soon he will set all things right. The lion reproaches the eagle for its injustice (11.40-42), confirms God's wrath against it (11.43-44), and predicts the eagle's utter destruction (11.45-46), and the burning of 'the whole body of the eagle' (12.3; compare the destruction of the body of the fourth beast in Dan. 7.11, whose body is engulfed with flames after its death). As a result, the whole earth will be freed of violence and oppression, so that it might be refreshed and relieved (11.46).

It is important to note, however, that the portrayal of evil's power and pervasiveness in episode V is depicted in a way that undermines any potential threat to the justice and sovereignty of God. Important here are the lion's words of 11.39, as it says to the eagle:

> Are you not the one that remains of the four beasts that I had made
> to reign in my world, so that the end of my times might come
> through them?

The evil reign of the eagle does not run contrary to God's sovereignty, but is shown to be included within God's own purposes in this world. The lion's words imply that evil must reach its climax before the arrival of God's new age (as was commonly held); the eagle's reign is merely a part of the final throes of this world (often referred to as the 'messianic woes') prior to the arrival of a new world where God reigns supreme. The eagle's rule may appear to be immutable and indestructible, but its

rule is permitted by the sovereign God who himself has established the
eagle's reign (11.39a) in order that evil might increase (implied) and
that, consequently, 'the end of my times might come' (11.39b). Here,
then, is a blurring of the divide between God and the forces of evil;
while evil is portrayed in sharp contrast to the will of God, it is
nonetheless depicted as falling within the scope of divine jurisdiction.
Evil is not to be located beyond the boundaries of God's justice, power
and control (as Ezra's complaints in episodes I-III implied) but lies
within the all-encompassing orbit of divine sovereignty. In true apocalyptic fashion, the author has interpreted the situation of his own day
within a theocentric perspective; the power and pervasiveness of evil
has been unmasked, revealing it as an unstable and temporary phenomenon that, in an ironic fashion, is serving to promote its own destruction prior to the final triumph of the sovereign God. The fact that God
reigns supreme is reinforced in 11.44 simply by the double reference to
'his' world.

There is a further indication that the eagle's reign is on course for
destruction, since in the last stages of its reign evil is depicted as being
at odds with itself, and the scaffolding of its edifice is shown to be
inherently fragile. As the reign of evil becomes more powerful (11.32;
12.24-25), so instability is shown to infiltrate its structures. This instability is represented in the later stages of the eagle's reign by the
devouring of one part of its body by another part (11.28-35), a veiled
reference to Roman leaders usurping other leaders in efforts to increase
their own stature and power. The successive rise of evil rulers is not an
indication that evil reigns supreme but, instead, depicts the existence of
a cancerous, self-destructive impulse within the structures of evil itself.
If Rome advertised itself to be a force for peace and order within this
world, the vision of episode V has revealed it to be a manifestation of
the chaotic forces of evil whose own power-base is being eroded by
the cancerous effects of chaos. The integrity of evil is disintegrating as
chaos floods its own ranks and rips them apart through internal
inchoate impulses. Although the primary theological conviction of this
vision is centred on the sovereignty of God who will overthrow the
forces of evil in this world, the depiction of evil at odds with itself in
11.28-35 is nonetheless an important study of the self-destructive
nature inherent within the forces of evil.

In the interpretation of this vision, the lion is explicitly identified
with the messiah (12.31-32). The imagery of the lion seems to be a
development of the imagery of Gen. 49.9:

Judah is a lion's whelp, from the prey, my son, you have gone up.
He stooped down he couched as a lion, and as a lioness; who dares
rouse him up?

The identification of the lion as the messiah compares with the imagery
in the Christian Apocalypse of John, where Jesus is depicted as the
'Lion of the tribe of Judah, the root of David' (Rev. 5.5). Davidic
descent is attributed to the messiah also in 4 Ezra 12.32, although he is
not portrayed in a royal or militaristic fashion. Instead, his function is
defined in images drawn from a court of law; he accuses Rome of its
atrocities (12.31-32), pronounces judgement in accordance with these
accusations (12.33), and carries out the judgement against Rome by
destroying it (12.34). Mention of the messiah having been 'kept until
the end of days' (12.32; cf. 13.26) seems to refer to the Jewish belief
that eschatological things have been created before the creation of the
this world and are simply being kept until God is ready to bring an end
to things as they are at present (cf. 4 Ezra 7.14, 70; 8.52, 59; 9.18; similarly, 3.6, where the Garden of Eden is said to have been planted by
God prior to the earth's own creation). It highlights his pre-existence,
but in no way is this thought of as being in tension with his Davidic
lineage. The kingdom of the messiah is not the climax or conclusion of
history; like Rome's own rule, the messiah's kingdom is shown to be
temporary with a fixed point for its end (12.34; cf. 7.28), prior to the
day of judgement, after which the new age is expected.

Episode V closes with reference to Ezra's location and diet. He is
said to be in a field where he waits for seven days eating only the
flowers of the field (12.51). Both of these features recall the end of
episode III, when Uriel instructed him to go out into a field and,
breaking his fast, to eat only the flowers of the field (9.23-24; cf. 9.26-
27). This change of diet and location preceded the transformation of
Ezra's attitude and demeanour. Mention of precisely the same two
factors, then, would seem to be an intentional signal that Ezra's
visionary experiences are part and parcel of the process of consolidation
that marks out the last half of the book. Expectations are raised, then,
with regard to the next episode in Ezra's journey.

The Man from the Sea Vision of Episode VI

Whereas the fifth episode develops the Danielic vision with reference
to the fourth kingdom mentioned in Dan. 7.7-8 and 7.11 (cf. 7.19-28),
the sixth episode develops the Danielic vision with reference to the

'one like a son of man' in Dan. 7.13-14. Whereas the messianic figure
is described in similar terms in both episodes, the culprit whom he
opposes in episode V is a specific manifestation of evil within the political sphere (Rome) while in episode VI the opposition that arises up
against him is from an innumerable 'multitude' (13.5, 9, 11, 28, 34)
comprising 'all the nations' of the earth (13.33) with a much more
universal, much less political focus. All their efforts of making war
against one another will be gathered together and directed against the
messiah (13.33); those who sought to remove each other from the
scene join together as one in a desperate effort to remove the divine
agent from this world.

The vision itself in 13.1-13a (apart from the interpretation) is much
easier to understand than the previous vision in 11.1–12.3a. Although
the vision proper of episode VI is not wholly transparent, nevertheless
it does not comprise the kind of involved and opaque symbolism that
characterized the earlier vision, and (to the modern eye anyway) it
demonstrates a simpler narrative flow than the vision of 11.1–12.3a.
This contrasts sharply also with the interpretation of the vision in
13.25-52, which has the appearance of several somewhat disjointed
strands of thought collected together.

The 'man' of episode VI (13.3, 5, 12, 25, 51) is a messianic figure,
who is also identified by God as 'my Son' in 13.32, 37, 52 (cf. 7.28–29;
14.9). The NRSV accepts the title 'my Son' as original, although some
think that a stronger case can be made for the title 'my servant' (cf.
Stone, *Fourth Ezra*, pp. 207-208). The textual issue is whether the
Latin term *filius* derives from a Greek υἱός which testifies to an original
Hebrew bn, in which case the translation should be 'son', or whether
the Latin derives from a Greek παῖς which testifies to an original
Hebrew 'bd, in which case the translation should be 'servant'. (This
reconstruction is dependent upon the accepted textual history of 4
Ezra, that a Hebrew original was translated into Greek from which the
extant translations all derive; see above, chapter 1). Either reading
might be of interest for scholars of early Christianity, since this passage
helps to demonstrate that there was within first-century Judaism a
consciousness of the messiah bearing one of these titles. Nonetheless,
caution needs to be exercised in this regard, since the content given to
either of these titles may differ in 4 Ezra from that given it in a
Christian context, where 'son' is associated with a gamut of ideas not
found here and where 'servant' seems to be ultimately indebted to the
portrait of the Ebed Yahweh ('Servant of God') in Deutero-Isaiah, a

phenomenon not immediately evident in 4 Ezra.

The messianic 'man' is a pre-existent being, as is clear from 13.26, 32 and 52 where he is said to have been kept hidden for many ages until the time of his appearing, a notion evident in episode V as well (12.32). These passages are not about a divine foreknowledge of the identity of the messiah long before such a human is ever born; instead, they refer to the pre-existence of the messiah himself, who is reserved in the wings of the stage of human history until the time when it is right for him to appear.

This divine being is depicted in imagery similar to that which is used to depict God in the Jewish scriptures and literature. So, for instance, the man from the sea appears (as did the Son of Man in Dan. 7.13) with clouds (13.3), just as the God of Israel is said to appear in clouds (Exod. 19.9; Num. 12.5; 1 Kgs 8.10-11) and to ride the clouds (Ps. 68.5; Isa. 19.1; Nah. 1.3) which serve as his chariot (Ps. 104.3). (Similar imagery appears elsewhere as well in the Christian Bible: Mk 9.7 parr.; Mk 13.26 parr.; Mk 14.61 parr.; Rev. 1.7.) The man's voice causes humans to melt like wax (13.4), just as the mountains melt like wax before God (4 Ezra 8.23; Ps. 97.5; Mic. 1.3-4; 1 En. 1.6) and as sinners do also (Pss. 68.2). The terrible gaze of the man, that causes everything to tremble, recalls the image of God's glance drying up the depths in 4 Ezra 8.23 and the words of Ps. 104.32 in relation to God: 'who looks on the earth and it trembles'. The man needs no weapons or instruments to carry out his defeat of those who oppose him (cf. also Pss. Sol. 17.33-34), since he brings about his victory by means of 'a stream of fire', 'a flaming breath' and 'a storm of sparks' from his tongue (13.10-11); this is reminiscent of the scriptural image of God, who 'burns up his adversaries round about' by means of fire (Ps. 97.3) and who executes judgement 'with flames of fire' (Isa. 66.15-16; cf. Ps. 18.9; 2 Sam. 22.9; Ezek. 39.6; Amos 1.4, 7, 10, 12, 14; 2.2, 5). It is interesting to note that, as the Syriac version alone testifies, the image of the destroying fire is interpreted in 13.38 to refer to 'the law', the instrument of the man's judgement against sinners; here one of the interests that characterizes the first three episodes has found its way into the author's interpretation of the traditional vision.

The primary significance of this episode is the same as that of episode V—granting assurance concerning the ultimate triumph of God and the deliverance of creation from the forces of evil that oppose God and run rampant throughout this world. But episode VI goes further than episode V in identifying those who will benefit from this future triumph. Episode V, focusing primarily on the destruction of Rome, makes mention of those who will benefit from the messiah's activity. They are a 'remnant of my people, those who have been saved throughout my borders' and whom the messiah makes joyful (12.34). This description has no relationship to the contents of the vision itself and seems to have been added to the interpretation of the vision by the author of 4 Ezra. These are the survivors of the messianic woes, who reappear in episode VI at the beginning and at the end of the angel's words to Ezra in the interpretation of the vision (13.21-24, 48-50), where they are described in similar terms: they 'are found within my holy borders' (13.48) and will be spared because of their 'works and faith [or better: 'faithfulness'] toward the Almighty' (13.23). All this echoes what Uriel said of this group earlier in episode III, where the survivors of the messianic woes are said to be spared 'on account of their works, or on account of the faith by which they have believed [or better: 'faithfulness in which they have put their trust']...and will see my salvation in my land and within my borders' (9.7-8). The messianic woes are the means whereby the righteous are differentiated from the wicked.

In episode VI, however, we are introduced to another group who, along with the remnant, will enjoy the benefits of the messianic age, a group never before mentioned in 4 Ezra, whether by Ezra or Uriel. In the vision itself, brief reference is made to a peaceable multitude who are gathered to the man (13.12). If this vision existed prior to the author's own use of it, it is likely that this mention of a gathered multitude was originally intended to refer to the ingathering of the diaspora Jews as they return to the land of their forefathers in the age when all is set aright. According to the author of 4 Ezra, however, the peaceable multitude becomes a symbol of the ten tribes of Israel who had gone into exile in another land (13.40-41), an event recorded in 2 Kgs 17.1-6. In the author's own elaborate depiction of this event, these ten tribes were not the pawns of a stronger nation that had exiled them; instead, they are said to have left their land by means of their own devising in order to 'leave the multitude of the nations and go to a more distant region, where no human beings had ever lived' (13.41). Their motivation behind all this was simply to keep the statutes of the law 'that they had not kept in their own land' (13.42). They are shown to have crossed the River Euphrates by means of divine intervention, and, because they have kept the statutes of the law in this distant land, so God will again intervene on their behalf and lead them back, gathering them in peace to enjoy the messianic age (13.47).

The question might arise, What really happened to the tribes that, according to the biblical account, were, in fact, exiled from their land and were never heard from again? Most likely, they would have assimilated the ways of their captors and lost their Jewish identity. Nonetheless, the belief that the ten tribes still existed 'beyond the Euphrates, countless myriads whose number cannot be ascertained' is evident from several Jewish writings of the time (Josephus, *Ant.* 11.33; *2 Bar.* 77.22, 78; cf. *m. Sanh.* 10.3), and the author of 4 Ezra is simply tapping into that belief and incorporating it into this eschatological vision.

A more appropriate question might be, What theological function does this tradition serve within the context of 4 Ezra? While it may provide a tidy explanation for an awkward event of Israel's past (the exile of the northern kingdom), it is not the author's concern to sew together the patches of Israel's history. Instead, the mention of the salvation of the ten tribes contributes to a different purpose here. First, it serves to reinforce a model of piety that the author is seeking to establish. These tribes have become the representatives of this ideal devotion to God, in which the demands of righteousness are determinative upon the whole of one's lifestyle. They have become the example of living in accordance with the will of God no matter the cost. They have recognized the seriousness of what loyalty to God entails, and have completely up-rooted their way of life in order to align themselves with the stipulations and expectations of God. Moreover, and significantly, they have done all this in a land far away, without recourse to the Jerusalem temple. The author of 4 Ezra might well have hoped that this reinterpretation of Jewish history would be instructive in the life of the late first-century post-destruction Jewish community.

A second possibility also arises when considering the function of this reworking of Israel's past in episode VI. It may well be that this reunion of the tribes of the northern kingdom with the remnant of the tribes of the southern kingdom is the author's own way of depicting the traditional Jewish hope that the eschatological future would involve the restoration of the twelve tribes of Israel, as salvation is granted to a single twelve-tribe conglomerate from within the complete ranks of the Jewish people. In this way, the traditional tribal composition of Jewish patriarchal history is maintained in the author's depiction of eschatological salvation, in accordance with traditional Jewish expectations. That the messiah is instrumental in all of this is not surprising; he facilitates the grand reunion of Israel by gathering together all those worthy to be included as members of God's people in the wonders of the messianic kingdom.

Almost as a miscellaneous note, it is interesting to observe that the messiah is depicted in slightly different ways in different contexts throughout the narrative of 4 Ezra (7.28-29; 11.37–12.1; 12.31-34; 13.3-13, 25-52; 14.9). In one context he is active (chs. 11–13), while in another he is inactive (7.28-29); in one context he appears after the revelation of the heavenly city and land (7.26-29), while in another he appears before it (chs. 11–13); in one context he condemns sinners (12.32), while in another he plays no role in relation to sinners (7.28-29); in one context he acts as a judge (12.31-34), while in another judgment follows long after he has died (7.28-44); in one context he has a political role (chs. 11–12), while in another his task carries no political significance (7.28-29). Evidently, various depictions are being culled from tradition and are allowed to sit alongside each other. This should caution us against thinking that there was a single, coherent and normative Jewish expectation concerning the messiah in early Jewish thought.

While recognizing the fluidity in the presentation of messianic ideas, one point deserves mention. Although it is often said that the messiah of 7.28 is a mortal human being, Michael Stone has argued that the reference there to the messiah being 'revealed' presupposes his pre-existence. If this is the case, it is interesting to note that, despite the lack of uniformity on other issues, the messiah is depicted consistently throughout the narrative as a pre-existent, heavenly being, despite the single (and unparalleled) reference to his death in 7.29.

While the messiah is not insubstantial to the author's theology, neither is he necessarily a crucial component of it. His place in the unfolding events of the eschaton is important in episodes V and VI (made up of largely traditional material), where he is shown to be the central agent of God in the events of the eschatological future; nonetheless, in some passages, the eschatological events are described without even a mention of a messianic figure (e.g. 6.18-29; 9.1-13), and elsewhere the messiah is mentioned incidentally, almost in passing, without filling up the whole of the eschatological drama (7.28-29). Throughout the narrative, the messiah and his kingdom are not depicted as everlasting but as temporary phenomena (7.29; 12.34); they are not the goal towards which all of history was directed, even if they are a welcome and significant step along the way.

The fourth part of episode VI concludes this grand vision with a commendation of the way in which Ezra has undergone a transformation in his understanding of God's ways (13.51-58). The consolation, for which he had longed but which had evaded him throughout the early episodes, he now fully enjoys, as a consequence of his transformation within the pages of the narrative. With the visions of episodes IV, V and VI, Ezra has been strengthened in his confidence and assurance of the justice and sovereignty of God. Accordingly, the episode ends in 13.57-8 with a portrait of Ezra unprecedented within the pages of 4 Ezra:

> Then I got up and walked in the field, giving great glory and praise to the Most High for the wonders that he does from time to time, and because he governs the times and whatever things come to pass in their seasons.

Further Reading

1. *On the visions of episodes V and VI*
A. Lacocque, 'The Vision of the Eagle in 4 Esdras: A Rereading of Daniel 7 in the First Century CE', in K.H. Richards (ed.), *SBL Seminar Papers 1981* (Chico, CA: Scholars Press, 1981), pp. 237-58. A somewhat unfocused article, showing how the scriptural text of Daniel 7 was being given new import. Lacocque, who does nothing with the remnant motif of the vision, concludes with an interesting suggestion as to how this vision might be relevant today.
H.C. Kee, ' "The Man" in Fourth Ezra: Growth of a Tradition', in K.H. Richards (ed.), *SBL Seminar Papers 1981*, pp. 199-208. Kee analyses how an independent tradition has been adapted in order to address particular circumstances within the life of an apocalyptic community; Kee's analysis of the social context of 4 Ezra, however, is much different from that adopted in chapter 8 below.
J.J. Collins, 'The Son of Man in First-Century Judaism', *NTS* 38 (1992), pp. 448-66, esp. 459-66. Collins demonstrates how Daniel 7 was understood in two first-century texts, 1 Enoch 37–71 and 4 Ezra 13, noting four common features.
G.K. Beale, *The Use of Daniel in Jewish Apocalyptic Literature and in the Revelation of St John* (Lanham, MD: University Press of America, 1984), pp. 112-44. An analysis of the influence of Daniel on the visions in 4 Ezra 11–13.

2. *On the messiah in 4 Ezra*
M.E. Stone, 'The Question of the Messiah in 4 Ezra', in J. Neusner *et al.* (eds.), *Judaisms and Their Messiahs* (Cambridge: Cambridge University Press,

1987), pp. 209-25. Stone analyses the relevant material, considers the function of the messiah in the author's theological project, and reflects upon the kind of social setting for which the messiah of 4 Ezra would be significant.

J.H. Charlesworth, 'From Jewish Messianology to Christian Christology: Some Caveats and Perspectives', in J. Neusner *et al.* (eds.), *Judaisms and Their Messiahs*, pp. 225-65, esp. 241-45. Charlesworth analyses the relevant material and considers the function of the messiah within the book.

3. *On Jewish messianism in general*

J. Neusuer *et al.*, *Judaisms and Their Messiahs*: A collection of essays examining the rise and role of messianic theology in early Jewish and Christian theology.

J.H. Charlesworth (ed.), *The Messiah* (Minneapolis: Fortress Press, 1992). An extensive collection of essays examining messianic figures and convictions in a wide range of Jewish and Christian literature.

EZRA, THE PEOPLE AND THE LAW
EPISODE VII

Ezra and Moses

The seventh and final episode of 4 Ezra is sometimes referred to as the epilogue of the book. In some senses, the word 'epilogue' is appropriate, for things are different enough in this episode that it might be thought to stand slightly apart from the six earlier episodes. Nowhere, for instance, does Uriel make an appearance in the seventh episode, as he has throughout all the previous episodes; now God himself converses with Ezra without mediation. At this point in Ezra's development, there is no longer the need for the angel who conversed with him (episodes I-III) or interpreted the visions for him (episodes IV-VI), for now God himself (in whose name the angel spoke) appears to Ezra. This difference helps to mark out the epilogue from the previous sections of the book. Nonetheless, the term 'epilogue' should not imply that this episode is an insignificant appendage that holds a secondary position to the earlier narrative. The author was not content to allow the narrative to conclude even on the zenith of Ezra's words of praise at the end of VI (13.57-58), and the seventh episode does more than simply provide the book with an aesthetically pleasing ending (the function stated by Gunkel). Instead, it develops the narrative further so that, while it does not continue in the same vein as the dialogues or visions of the previous six episodes, it is nonetheless essential to the development of the book, especially in its depiction of the law and related matters.

A first indication of the essential place of this episode within the broader narrative is evident from its first four words: 'On the third day' (14.1). Every episode except the first has begun with a temporal signifier of this sort, but this one is significant in helping to establish a topological relationship between Ezra and Moses, an important aspect of the final episode of 4 Ezra. This is evident first by means of a simple count of the days that have passed since Ezra's whole enterprise began. In 4 Ezra 6.35 we are told of 'three weeks' that have passed, referring to three seven-day fasts that Ezra underwent: one between episodes I and II (5.20-21), another between episodes II and III (6.31, 35), and another (although unrecorded) is assumed to have happened prior to episode I. After these twenty-one days, we are told of another seven-day period between episodes III and IV (9.23, 27), a two-day period between episodes IV and V (10.58; 11.1), a seven-day period between episodes V and VI (12.39; 13.1), and a three-day period between episodes VI and VII (13.56, 58; 14.1). These add up to a period of forty days, the same number of days in which God revealed himself to Moses on Mount Sinai. As others have shown, the author seems to have taken great care in constructing the passage of time within his narrative, and to have arranged the temporal aspect of Ezra's progress in order that, in this final episode, the parallels between Moses and Ezra might emerge clearly (see Knowles, 'Moses'; Stone, *Fourth Ezra*, pp. 373-74). The same point is reinforced in 14.23 and 14.36, where another period of forty days is mentioned, during which time Ezra receives divine revelation from God in order to write down in books all that God wishes to reveal.

That this close identification of Ezra and Moses is an important matter at this point in the narrative can be demonstrated further in 14.1-2. If the episode begins with Ezra sitting, he does not keep this position for long. Instead, he rises to his feet (the posture he has adopted at times of special importance) as God himself comes to him and speaks from within a bush. This is patterned on the encounter between Moses and God in Exodus 3, as is made explicit in 4 Ezra 14.3: 'I revealed myself in a bush and spoke to Moses'. Further parallels between the biblical account and this one include calling the human twice by name ('Moses, Moses'; 'Ezra, Ezra') and the form of response to God in the words 'here I am' (Exod. 3.4; 4 Ezra 14.2; cf. Gen. 22.11; 1 Sam. 3.10). By means of such twin patterning, the author seeks to establish strong relational links between the two figures, a relationship not developed earlier in the book.

One subsidiary point might also be made in this regard. In the same way that episodes V and VI reverberate with meaning drawn from the symbolic world of Daniel 7 (as noted above in chapter 6), so too it might be that echoes of meaning reverberate within the early stages of episode VII from the symbolic world of Exodus 3 in relation to the deliverance of the Hebrew people from their oppressive bondage in Egypt. It may be significant to note that, in Ezra's final address to the people in 14.27-36, the first thing that is recalled is the enslavement and liberation of the Hebrew people from Egypt (14.29). This follows God's own lead in 14.3-4 as he addresses Ezra, recalling the same biblical episode:

> I revealed myself in a bush and spoke to Moses when my people were in bondage in Egypt: and I sent him and led my people out of Egypt.

So the biblical account of the exodus is twice referred to in this final episode (compare the double elaboration of Daniel 7 in episodes V and VI), almost as if that event were acting as an implicit precedent to the situation in which the people of Israel found themselves in the author's day. Moreover, the next few verses recall God's revelation to Moses of 'many wondrous things' on Mount Sinai and his commissioning of Moses to publish these things (14.4-6); a similar revelation and commission is soon to take place for Ezra who, like Moses of old, is to comfort the people in their distress and gather them together around the Torah. It might be, then, that the author of 4 Ezra intended lines of comparison to be drawn not only between Moses and Ezra but also between ancient Hebrew people and the people of Israel in the late first century CE. In this case, a topological relationship would be assumed between the enslavement of the Hebrews to the super-power Egypt and the context of the people of Israel in the author's own day in relation to the super-power Rome. The deliverance of the Hebrews from Egypt formed the basis of Israel's collective self-identity as a people, and it may be that the author of 4 Ezra intends to tap into that powerful precursive story in order to bolster a sense of hopefulness and confidence for the Jewish people of his own day; the present perplexing situation is to be redressed, just as the exodus of old transformed the misfortune of the Hebrews into a glorious result.

If such links are implicit in this episode, they are nonetheless secondary to the more fundamental topological relationship between Ezra and Moses established by the author. The function of this relationship is especially important later in the episode, when Ezra is inspired by God to receive and write the divine revelation in two forms: he is to reveal the law to the people in general, and to reveal other books of wisdom and understanding to the wise in particular. In

this regard, Ezra is not depicted as simply a scribe of the law, nor as one
in a long line of prophets. Although Ezra has had a prophetic identity
throughout the first six episodes (cf. 5.16-20; 12.40-51, esp. 12.42), he
now takes on a new identity, and one that transforms him in his role.
So, Ezra's authority is shown not to depend upon an inherited
authority from Moses; instead, he becomes a new Moses figure, who is
directly inspired by God to carry out his task (14.25, 38-43). This
experience of divine inspiration, through which the people are given
the law and the wise are granted instruction in wisdom and understanding, is neither divergent from nor subject to Moses' authority.
As will be shown below, this focus on authority and revelation is
important especially with regard to the seventy books that are to be
distributed privately.

Ezra, the People and the Torah

As part of his divinely commissioned task, Ezra is instructed to 'reprove
your people' and to 'comfort the lowly among them' (14.13). This he
carries out in the last of his public words in 14.27-36, when he
instructs all the people of Israel.

A similar situation is evident in the last part of episode V, when all
the people gather around Ezra to discover how his deliberations were
proceeding on their behalf. The despair of the people is evident
throughout 12.40-45, as they articulate their feelings of despondent
desperation, giving voice to the sentiment that, without hope, life itself
is meaningless:

> Therefore if you forsake us, how much better it would have been for
> us if we also had been consumed in the burning of Zion. (12.44)

Their tone and sentiment is reminiscent of Ezra's throughout the first
three episodes, as is especially clear from 4.12:

> It would have been better for us not to be here than to come here
> and live in ungodliness, and to suffer and not understand why.

So too it is reminiscent of the attitude of the woman in episode IV,
whose disheartened misery led her to wish for her own death.

Throughout 4 Ezra, Ezra has made a pilgrimage in relation to his
own feelings of despair. In the early episodes, his grief threatened to
undermine his confidence in God's sovereignty. In episode IV,
however, Ezra demonstrated a new attitude in which heartfelt grief was
offset by certainty in the justice of God. Consequently, in that episode

Ezra could attempt to uproot the despair of the woman and to comfort her, just as in episode V he takes up the same task in relation to all the people of Israel who come to him in desperation.

> Take courage, O Israel; and do not be sorrowful, O house of Jacob; for the Most High has you in remembrance, and the Mighty One has not forgotten you in your struggle. (12.36-37)

This contrasts with Ezra's rather brisk handling of Phaltiel who pleaded on Israel's behalf in 5.16-19, but who received from Ezra no word of comfort. By episode V, however, Ezra can act as the comforter of the people because he has allowed himself to accept that God is just (episode IV) and because he has received comfort from the vision of episode V (cf. 12.8), which revealed that God will act in the end to defeat evil and set things right. His comforting of the people in this same episode emerges from this conviction that God is in control. All this is in stark contrast to the Ezra of the early episodes, who was tormented in mind and spirit because of the fact that the righteous sovereignty of God looked to be threatened by the events of this world of evil.

The same is true of Ezra's encounter with the people in episode VII. Having concluded the sixth episode with exultant strains of praise for all that God has done and will do, Ezra is qualified to comfort the people prior to his departure from this world. His parting words to the people confirm yet again that Ezra is not the same person that he was in the early episodes. Although he reviews many of the same events of Israel's history as he did in his opening speech of episode I, his point here is much different. In his speech of 3.4-36 Ezra charged God with injustice; the people's failure to keep the law revealed a more fundamental failure on God's part since he had neglected to act decisively on their behalf. In this final episode, however, Ezra affirms that God 'is a righteous judge' (14.32) and that the responsibility for the people's condition rests wholly with them, since they, like their forefathers, have failed to keep the law (14.28-31). In view of the final judgement that awaits everyone after death, Ezra charges them to 'rule over your minds and discipline your hearts' (14.34).

Complaint against God, long since abandoned by Ezra, has no place in any of this, and in its stead stands complete confidence in God. It is also important to note that Ezra conveys no sense of pessimism to the people about the possibility of overcoming sin and fulfilling the law, as his words in 14.34 demonstrate; this is reminiscent of Uriel's view throughout the early episodes (see, e.g., 7.20-24, 92, 127-28). In his address to the people, Ezra speaks of the law as a 'law of life' (14.30; cf. 14.22; 9.31, 37).

The restoration of the law becomes a central issue in episode VII since, as Ezra says in 14.21, it has been destroyed in the demolition of the city (cf. 4.23). The law is to be restored in order that all succeeding generations might observe it and 'find the path' (14.22). The law is instructive for all time. As 4 Ezra nears its end, the reader is given a description of the extraordinary manner in which the law was recorded. Ezra became divinely inspired by drinking a fire-like liquid that enlivened his understanding, causing him to speak for forty days; during that period, Ezra's five scribes became similarly inspired and miraculously wrote his words 'using characters that they did not know' (14.42; that is, they wrote in the square characters [Aramaic] which, according to tradition, came into existence in Ezra's day).

The result of all this activity was the production of ninety-four books divided into two classes: one group of twenty-four books, and another of seventy books. The identification of the twenty-four books is not problematic, since they no doubt refer to the books of the Hebrew scriptures, which number twenty-four in Jewish tradition. Both the worthy and the unworthy are allowed to read them. The identification of the seventy books will be discussed below. Ezra is commanded to make the twenty-four books of the law available to the people, to 'the worthy and the unworthy' (14.45). All this follows from Ezra's conviction, expressed in 14.20-22, that the law never becomes obsolete and out-dated, but remains permanently valid for every generation.

The Law and the Seventy Books

The long narrative of 4 Ezra closes with a final instruction from God to Ezra:

> Make public the twenty-four books that you wrote first, and let the worthy and the unworthy read them; but keep the seventy that were written last, in order to give them to the wise among your people. For in them [the seventy books] is the spring of understanding, the fountain of wisdom, and the river of knowledge. (14.45-47)

The Latin manuscripts of 4 Ezra close with Ezra's statement 'And I did so' in 14.48, but it is probable that the original narrative ended with a brief account in 14.49-50 of Ezra's assumption into heaven where he lives with the messiah and the elect (cited by the nrsv in a footnote, suggesting that this is an addition in the Syriac manuscript rather than original to the text).

A proper identification of the seventy books mentioned here is important. On occasion it has been suggested that they represent the Jewish oral tradition that was developing and that later became codified in the Mishnah and other rabbinic texts. In this view, the author is attributing divine origin and authority to both the written and the oral law. More commonly, the seventy books are identified as the large corpus of Jewish apocalyptic texts—in particular, those apocalyptic texts which, like 4 Ezra itself, depict the events of the end times. It is probably too much, however, to believe that the author was thinking at this point of a specific library of books belonging to some guild of eschatological seers; he is not interested in legitimating some corpus of apocalyptic texts known to him, so even this interpretation of the seventy books probably deserves a more precise definition. The seventy books seem to be representative not of a library of texts but, as in 12.37-38, of eschatological mysteries. Whereas the biblical figure Ezra is known to have restored the Torah to the people, the text of 4 Ezra reveals that this second Moses figure also secretly propagated the mysteries of the end times that are the exclusive property of a select group of wise and learned men (compare the reception of secret revelations by Abraham and Moses in 3.14 and 14.5). Accordingly, the author of 4 Ezra seems to be authenticating the kind of elaborate eschatological enterprise evident in 4 Ezra and the majority of other Jewish apocalypses, even if he is not authenticating specific apocalyptic texts themselves.

It seems, then, that the number seventy is not to be understood as a literal signifier of the accumulated texts in some apocalyptic library; instead, it serves more of a symbolic function, signifying the quality or character of eschatological interests. The symbolism of the number 'seventy' can be understood as involving a play on the numerical value of the letters of the Hebrew word for 'secret' (*swd*), which add up to seventy ($s = 60$, $w = 6$, $d = 4$), (remembering that 4 Ezra seems originally to have been composed in Hebrew). This suggestion may look somewhat unusual to the modern mind, but this kind of numerical symbolism was often employed by ancient Jewish apocalypticists and was a common rhetorical technique in Early Judaism, making appearances within the New Testament as well (e.g., the 666 in Rev. 13.18 as the numerical value of the name of the Roman emperor Nero; the three groups of fourteen generations in Mt. 1.1-17, where Jesus is identified as the son of David, the numerical value of whose name adds up to fourteen). One piece of ancient graffiti reads: 'I love her whose name is 545', cryptically identifying the woman by the numerical equivalent of her name.

If similar symbolism is operative in 4 Ezra 14, the number 'seventy' would serve as a numerical code signifying the character of the eschatological mysteries. To arrive at a complementary number to twenty-four, the author simply translated the quality of these eschatological interests (that it, their secret character) into a numerical value (that is, seventy). In this view, the seventy books may function simply as a numeric metaphor reinforcing the point emphasized both in episode VII (14.26, 46; cf. 14.5-6) and in episode V (12.37-38) that knowledge of the way that God will act in the culmination of this age is to be a secret to all except the few who are 'wise' within Israel.

This association of the eschatological secrets with the few who are wise couples with a significant claim made for the seventy books in comparison with the twenty-four others. Whereas God reveals to Ezra that the twenty-four books of scripture are available to the worthy and the unworthy alike, the seventy books that are available only to the wise are alone said to contain 'the spirit of understanding, the fountain of wisdom, and the river of knowledge' (14.47). This characterization of the seventy books allows for an easy comparison of the way the books of the law are characterized by Moses in Deut. 4.6 as he instructs the people to follow the laws of God:

> For this will show your wisdom and understanding to the nations,
> who will hear about all these decrees and say, 'Surely this great
> nation is a wise and understanding people'.

This connection between wisdom and the Torah is well established in Jewish scripture and literature (e.g., Ps. 119.97-100; Sir. 19.20; 24.6-8, 23; Bar. 3.36-4.4; 2 Bar. 38.2, 4; 48.22-23; 54.5; T. Levi 4.3-5), and has already been stated by Ezra in 4 Ezra 8.12.

In 4 Ezra 14, however, a different scenario appears. Despite Moses' coupling of wisdom with the law in Deut. 4.6, the author of 4 Ezra is convinced that only the wisdom of the seventy secret books is able to make sense of human experience in the light of the tragic events of 70 CE. The few who are educated in wisdom do not meditate exclusively on the law but, more importantly, on the secrets of God's eschatological ways. Whereas the law is given to all as their path to life, the eschatological mysteries address the conundrums of human existence that Ezra has examined in the earlier episodes by placing them within the theocentric context of the ultimate triumph of God. The secrets concerning the end times may be consonant with the Mosaic law, but they also exceed its boundaries and provide the interpretative key for any curious anomalies within history by placing those anomalies within a secure framework of confidence in God's ultimate triumph. Why these should be classified matters, concealed from the general public, will be considered in the next chapter when considering the author's purposes in writing 4 Ezra. In retrospect, the casting of Ezra in the garb of a second Moses throughout this episode allows great authority to be granted to the kind of eschatological matters that have proven to be so significant in Ezra's search for understanding and consolation.

Further Reading

Attitudes towards scripture in Jewish apocalyptic writings

M.A. Knibb, 'Apocalyptic and Wisdom in 4 Ezra', *JSJ* 13 (1982), pp. 56-74. The relationship between the private and public distinction in 4 Ezra is considered (pp. 62-65), followed by a demonstration of the influence of scripture on the author, in particular the influence of Job, Genesis and Daniel (pp. 65-72).

C. Rowland, 'Apocalyptic Literature', in D.A. Carson and H.G.M. Williamson (eds.), *It is Written: Scripture Citing Scripture* (Cambridge: Cambridge University Press, 1988), pp. 170-89. 4 Ezra 14 plays an important role in his helpful analysis of the relationship between scripture and apocalyptic literature, demonstrating how Jewish apocalypticists understood their enterprise to be a product of their immersion in the texts of scripture.

D. Patte, *Early Jewish Hermeneutic in Palestine* (Missoula: Scholars Press, 1975), pp. 131-208. The Jewish apocalypticists thought of themselves as supplementing scripture, which was otherwise incomplete. 4 Ezra is not studied, but this survey provides interesting parallels with 4 Ezra 14.

M.E. Stone, 'Apocalyptic—Vision or Hallucination?', *Milla wa-Milla* 14 (1974), pp. 47-56; now appears in his *Selected Studies in Pseudepigrapha and Apocrypha*, pp. 419-28. The pseudepigraphic nature of Jewish apocalypses reveals a consciousness of inspiration that allows apocalyptic authors to view their apocalyptic traditions as on a par with, and sometimes superseding, scripture. 4 Ezra is considered on pp. 423-24.

8

THE AUTHOR AND HIS THEOLOGICAL PROJECT

The Author's Theological Inquiry

At this point, it is necessary to assemble a synthesis of what we have seen, standing back from the separate parts of the text and seeing it as a single, well-composed entity by a considered author. It is important at the outset to note a feature of his presentation that has not been brought out within this guide but which would be evident from the commentaries. That is, throughout the narrative, the author demonstrates himself to be fully immersed in the resources of the Jewish scriptures. Although scriptural quotations are rare in 4 Ezra, allusions to scripture and its imagery are frequent, and in places the author seems to be consciously building on scriptural sources and hoping that echoes of scripture will resound within the context of the narrative. The author's theological concerns are informed by his familiar reading of scripture in relation to his experience.

The task of reconstructing the author's theological profile is complicated by two factors: (1) the dialogical nature of the text, in which two characters early on express viewpoints that are at odds with one another, and (2) the seven-episode structure of the book, that contains within itself a mid-point transformation of the main character. An assessment of the 'theology' of the text in relation to its author needs, therefore, to be carried out carefully and with sensitivity to these two fundamental characteristics of the narrative.

Ultimately, 4 Ezra might best be described as an affirmation of God's justice and sovereignty. This is what Ezra consistently questions and Uriel consistently affirms throughout the early episodes, what the visions of episodes IV to VI graphically depict, and what Ezra both presupposes and declares in his final instructions to the people. The Ezra of the second half of the book assimilates confidence in this affirmation not by means of rational enquiry but by a volitional decision to subscribe to the assessment of God as the benevolent and righteous sovereign of this world, a decision that receives validation in Ezra's overwhelming experience of seeing (by means of apocalyptic revelation) the events of the final eradication of evil and the triumph of God.

And yet, if this confident note is struck in the final four episodes, the same is not evident from the first three episodes, which comprise about sixty per cent of the book. This early section is marked out by its tone of frustration and despondency, as Ezra articulates the confusion of the people and receives solutions that seem inadequate to him, even if they issue from the mouth of a divine agent of God. If Ezra maintains that divine grace is the primary ingredient in the salvific recipe, Uriel maintains that God has done enough to rectify the situation of human sinfulness by giving the law to instruct those who choose to obey it. Uriel puts emphasis on personal responsibility to overcome the common fate of humanity, rather than on divine responsibility to take further initiatives. Ezra cannot accept Uriel's position, since it seems to him to go directly against the grain of the scriptural record of God's merciful dealings with Israel in covenant relationship. The law may have been gloriously given by God, but the people must be permitted to rely upon God's grace in this age.

In episode III, two main consequences follow from this discussion. First, without recourse to divine grace in the present, Ezra's initial exclusive concern for the people of Israel is shown to be inappropriate and inadequate, giving way to a more fundamental issue: the desperate situation of the whole of humanity. Second, without recourse to divine grace in the present, salvation can only be a glorious prospect for relatively few, since the force of sin has grabbed almost everyone up within its grasp. If divine grace is subordinate to the pre-determined plan for the unfolding of the ages, the consequences both for Israel and for humanity in general are desperately tragic.

The narrative of 4 Ezra allows two perspectives to tussle in the encounter between Ezra and Uriel, and neither perspective can be said to get the upper hand in their dialogues. Yet, in episode IV, a resolution begins to emerge as Ezra internalizes and articulates the sentiments that Uriel had voiced earlier, affirming the justice of God without complaint. Ezra's transformation has come about not by means of rational deduction but by a decision of the will to embrace what falls

beyond the boundaries of human knowledge and to accept that God is
righteous. This decision is then fortified and authenticated by means of
a vision of the heavenly city and by the eschatological visions of
episodes V and VI. In the final episode, the giving of the law to the
people takes place within the context of complete confidence in God's
justice, as if to suggest that such confidence and hope is the prerequisite
empowering and promoting faithfulness to the law in order to inherit
God's magnificent salvation.

In his book *The Story of the Other Wise Man*, Henry van Dyke has
one of his characters speak this proverb: 'religion without a great hope
would be like an altar without a living fire' (London: Harper &
Brothers [1895], p. 14). This, in a nutshell, might also capture the heart
of the author's theological interests. In strong and emotive images he
depicts the crippling effect of despair upon Ezra in episodes I-III and
on the mourning woman of episode IV, both of whom are caught up
in a perpetual downward spiral of hopelessness out of which little can
be salvaged. On the other hand, the overpowering images of the
second half of the book demonstrate the positive transformation that
results when one is animated by an attitude of confident hope, which
stimulates faithfulness, out of which regeneration arises, in which lies
the hope of salvation.

But, in this story of hopefulness, the Ezra of the early episodes is not
simply a figure of despair, for his despair arises out of his disappoint-
ment in explaining the anomalies between Israel's experience and her
inherited belief system concerning a gracious God. The tremendous
agony of Ezra in the dialogues is heartfelt and stirring, and his questions
are perceptive and penetrating. Uriel's responses, conversely, are often
insipid and fail to satisfy Ezra's intellectual and emotional quest. The
irony is that, although the reader's sympathies are expected to be with
Ezra in these early episodes, nonetheless the reader watches as a new
Ezra emerges full of confidence, hope and praise in the latter episodes.
Ezra's transformation is no doubt meant to be instructive for the reader,
who is to follow Ezra's lead in this process.

Moreover, this same process of transformation is likely to be indicative of the author's own spiritual progress. In this way, Ezra and Uriel
seem to represent two aspects in the author's own religious development. It may be somewhat simplistic to identify Ezra as the voice of
doubt and Uriel as the voice of faith, as is commonly done, for what
distinguishes the two primarily is a different fundamental conviction.
The faith of the early Ezra is marked out by the axiomatic conviction

that divine activity in this world is the product of God's gracious and merciful character. Uriel's perspective, which Ezra seems later to accept, is marked out by the underlying conviction that God's activity is determined by the divinely pre-ordained timetable of history, and that hope lies not in divine grace in the present but in the dramatic in-breaking of God in the final stages of this age and in the next. The other differences between the early Ezra and Uriel follow on from this more fundamental point, and the theological content of these two perspectives represent two packages of theological conviction and expectation at respective stages in the author's pilgrimage of theological reflection in relation to experience.

There is, then, a strong theological dynamic within the book, and the transformation that takes place there cannot be reduced simply to a psychological one. A theological case is being put forward in relation to traditional views concerning divine activity. 4 Ezra is not simply one man's exercise in wishful thinking. Nonetheless, this important theological dynamic of the book succeeds only in relation to its psychological dynamic. That is, the theological transformation presupposes a psychological (or better, perhaps, spiritual) one. So, although the visions of the second half of the text reinforce Ezra's theological transformation, their effectiveness is indebted to the fact that Ezra has already undergone a prior psychological transformation. The later episodes are able to fortify Ezra's confidence simply because he has already made the decision to stop complaining and to affirm God's justice. In some ways, then, Ezra's profound interrogations and protests earlier seem more to be side-stepped than tackled head-on in the later episodes. If the visions of the second half of the book address his earlier concerns, they address them not by rational proofs but by emotive and overpowering experiences that instil in Ezra an attitude of pious fear before God (10.25-37; 12.3b-6; 13.13b-15); if they are effective, their effectiveness is due to a prior commitment on Ezra's part early in episode IV simply to trust in the righteousness of God.

The text of 4 Ezra, then, may not succeed, in the end, in providing theological solutions to one of the most pressing and perennial theological conundrums of all time—the problem of reconciling the pervasive and destructive power of evil with the existence of a loving, just and sovereign God. The author himself seems aware of his failure in this regard, for the transformation of his main character comes about not by rational persuasion but by volitional metamorphosis (perhaps even off-stage, if Ezra shows signs of transformation already at 9.26-37, as I

argued above). In this regard, the author of 4 Ezra is little different
from the many others who have wrestled with this grand problem and
arrived at a less than satisfactory rational solution. No doubt, the
'problem of evil' will continue to be a problem as long as evil and
suffering continue to exist in this world. So too, one might be excused
for supposing that the grand and intricate rational theories of the
theodicist concerning the existence of evil in God's world may well fail
to reach the depths of personal despair and suffering at times of
immense heart-felt pain.

Presumably, the author of 4 Ezra has found the same to be true in
his own experience. Nonetheless, he refused to abandon his confidence
in God's justice and sovereignty. Was this due simply to a failure of
nerve on his part, or to some other impulse or conviction? Or to put
the question slightly differently: Is theodicy merely a rational exercise,
or might it not span several levels of one's personality? Some may look
upon 4 Ezra simply as an example of schizophrenic tension between
faith and doubt, a tension resolved in favour of faith only by the rather
paltry means of short-circuiting intellectual inquiry and pulling one's
self up by one's own psychological bootstraps. The fact that a rationally
adequate solution to the problem of evil may never be forthcoming
might lead some to conclude that traditional belief in God is woefully
off the mark. Or perhaps, if religious commitment has any merit, it
must be in a form that does not postulate an intimate connection
between the divine being and this world of suffering (so, for instance,
religions such as Buddhism or Hinduism). For others, however, it may
be that an inadequate rational solution does not lead to the abandon-
ment of fundamental religious convictions. For such people, theodicy is
not so much an enterprise of rational propositions and reasoned explanation, but a practical exercise carried out by those sorrowful in heart
who open themselves to the mystery of God and therein find healing
and restoration. It seems that the author of 4 Ezra is one such as these,
and this conviction, rather than any point in his theological repertoire,
may prove to be his greatest theological contribution.

The Consequences for Covenant Theology

We are now in a position to evaluate an issue first raised in chapter 2
above—the author's position in relation to the kind of covenant
theology that pervaded most forms of Judaism. This issue has been
lurking throughout our analysis of the text, but a full discussion of it

has been postponed until the survey of the text was complete.

In the second chapter of this guide, three positions were spelled out that can be said to characterize scholarly views on the author's handling of covenant theology, these positions having been labelled 'covenantal confirmation', 'covenantal redefinition', and 'covenantal abrogation'. Before considering this issue further, however, it needs to be noted that the process of categorization can often lead to over-simplification and misrepresentation; as long as this synthetic and somewhat artificial quality of the process is recognized, the exercise itself might help to further understanding.

Despite the claims of several scholars (among whom I previously counted myself), it seems inappropriate to identify a covenantal abrogation in 4 Ezra. Such a view seems to result from over-emphasizing certain aspects of the text at the expense of others. 4 Ezra might be compared to a tapestry of rich and diverse colour; to draw out only a particular strand of colour from that tapestry leaves behind a somewhat monochrome imitation of the real thing. It may well be that, in 4 Ezra, some central aspects of traditional covenantal expectation have been moved to the periphery of things, due to the divinely ordained scheme of the ages, and it may be that the original reader was expected to emerge with a redefined and modified covenant theology, but it would be going too far to say that a theology of covenant relationship is alto-gether abrogated in 4 Ezra. Such a view might build upon certain developments within 4 Ezra, but it nonetheless does not do justice to the full dynamics, tone and intent of the text.

Much the same might be said of the opposite view, that 4 Ezra simply confirms God's covenant fidelity to ethnic Israel, albeit with an eschatological modification. This view does justice to the enormous confidence in God that characterizes the second half of the book, and it has in its favour the grand scene in episode VI depicting the salvation of a twelve-tribe conglomerate. Nonetheless, it underplays the rather discouraging prospect that emerges with regard to most of the Jewish people; if Uriel maintained that only a few will be saved while most of the human race will be destroyed, even Ezra accepts this without complaint in episode IV (10.10). Moreover, in Uriel's interpretation of the visions in episodes V and VI, Ezra learns of the salvation of a remnant by the messiah; these survivors of the messianic woes are presumably (members of) the righteous few who will inherit the next age. (Compare the way in which Uriel's mention of the remnant who survive the messianic woes in 9.7-8 leads into Ezra's final disgruntled complaint about the salvation of only the few in 9.14-16.) Despite the influx of confidence in God in the later episodes, there does not seem to be an alleviation of Uriel's rigorous view throughout the early episodes. Neither does the mention of the salvation of the departed tribes in episode VI contradict this, for while it contributes to the confident tone of the later sections, there is little in it that might comfort and encourage the Jews of the late first century; it serves primarily as pedagogical instruction, an example of the kind of diligent faithfulness that God expects and that they should imitate, but it includes no assurances that God will deliver them in particular.

It seems, then, that the category which best describes the author's thought in this matter is that of covenantal redefinition. On the one hand, 4 Ezra shows itself to be animated by a covenant theology; on the other hand, this theological lens has been adapted and redefined in such a way that the benefits of the covenant have been restricted to the ranks of exceptional people, and traditional notions such as atonement and divine mercy are practically vacuous. Confidence in God's justice and faithfulness is the mainstay of the author's covenantal perspective, but it is a perspective that seems to be characterized by two other factors: (1) a somewhat sceptical attitude towards the people's ability to keep the law with the kind of rigorous and exacting standards that are required, and (2) the virtual absence of a robust theology of grace. While refusing to compromise his loyalty to and confidence in the God of the law and of Israel, the author has had to abandon his belief in one of the characteristic qualities of that God: graciousness. Instead, the God depicted in 4 Ezra is primarily one of power and of justice, and hope emerges from a consciousness of these attributes rather than from a consciousness of God's gracious working in the present age. In 4 Ezra, the demanding and arduous requirements expected of human beings are brought centre stage, leaving a full-bodied confidence in divine grace waiting in the wings. The God who brings down the curtain on this stage of history is one who triumphs over evil in power and who passes judgement upon all justly. Therein rests the hope of those who would seek to be faithful to God in covenant relationship.

The Social Setting of 4 Ezra

If we can delineate the author's theological profile along the lines given above, it is natural to consider the setting in which he wrote. Presumably, he wrote not simply for his own edification but in order to influence others. So we can ask about the text's social setting (here) and its social function (below). Such an inquiry is, by its very nature, a somewhat speculative enterprise, and this is especially true for 4 Ezra, which does not easily yield its secrets in this regard. Social indicators within the text are not at all obvious, and it is difficult to know where to begin when considering its position within a particular situation.

Some scholars speak of 4 Ezra in relation to a religious community, written by one member of that community to benefit that community. Since this much is probably true of most religious texts to one extent or another, the character, scope and interests of that community need to be identified. Perhaps the community to which 4 Ezra is addressed is a rather small, tightly-knit factional group within the umbrella of Judaism, whose members had close ties with each other but who were somewhat alienated from more mainstream forms of Judaism. This is the impression given, for instance, by H.C. Kee (see his 'The Man', listed below), who suggests that the author was a member of an apocalyptic community that considered itself to be the faithful remnant of Israel, while the rest of the people had been led astray by unfaithful leaders. The same impression is given by Kee's doctoral student, J.A. Overman. According to Overman, 4 Ezra is the text of a sectarian community, the members of which considered themselves to be the righteous remnant because of their faithfulness before God, while the rest of the people, especially those in power, had fallen away from God's law (see his *Matthew's Gospel*, listed below).

Reconstructions of this sort are attractive in their simplicity, and have parallels with reconstructions of other early Jewish texts. There are, however, serious difficulties that beset the kind of approach taken by Kee and Overman. Perhaps the most pressing obstacle to their view is the fact that 4 Ezra was not circulated within a closed or restricted context in the backwater of Jewish life. 4 Ezra shows strong theological connections with Pseudo-Philo's Biblical Antiquities (or LAB), and it shares similar theological concerns of theodicy as two other Jewish apocalypses in the post-destruction context: the Apocalypse of Abraham and 2 Baruch. Each of these three texts (Pseudo-Philo, the Apocalypse of Abraham and 2 Baruch) are well-situated within the mainstream of Jewish life. In fact, the relationship between 4 Ezra and 2 Baruch is especially close, with one text being a direct response to the other. (The present consensus tends to favour 2 Baruch being a response to 4 Ezra, asking similar questions in a less pointed fashion and affirming God's covenant faithfulness to Israel throughout in a much more confident and reassuring manner.) It is unlikely, then, that 4 Ezra could have been written in an alienated Jewish community if it holds a pivotal position within the literary relationship of these important texts. 4 Ezra is to be located more centrally within the spectrum of Jewish life in the first century than the 'sectarian' reconstruction allows.

If this is the case, one view that has often been advocated deserves serious consideration: that is, the author was a Jewish leader working within the post-destruction context in an attempt to reformulate Judaism without recourse to the temple. So, for instance, L.L. Grabbe, setting out some parameters for the study of the social setting of 4 Ezra, has considered whether or not the author might have been 'a Yavnean rabbi', a Jewish leader participating in the didactic activity at Yavneh. Without excluding other options, Grabbe concludes that this scenario is quite possible (see his 'Chronography', listed below).

In a later article, Grabbe looks at the social setting of Jewish apoca- lypticism in general, and challenges the notion that apocalypses neces- sarily arise from disenfranchised communities. Drawing on sociological and anthropological studies, Grabbe makes various proposals, including the suggestion that some apocalypses were composed by individual scribes or priests rather than by a factional apocalyptic community. According to Grabbe, apocalyptic writing was not foreign to the intel- ligentsia or leadership of society (see his 'Apocalypticism', listed below). The same point has been compellingly argued by P.R. Davies, who demonstrates that apocalyptic ideas are not necessarily 'counter-estab- lishment', and that the writing of apocalypses was most likely the activity of the intellectual and religious scribal elite. According to Davies, the apocalyptic genre may have been a kind of 'inner-scribal game' which, in interpreting the signs of the times, became an impor- tant pedagogical tool in the instruction of the people (see his 'Social World', listed below).

These studies cohere well with M. Knibb's work on 4 Ezra in particular. Knibb thinks 4 Ezra to be a work produced for a group of learned men whose perceptions have been formed from their study of the scriptures and who were engaged in interpretative writing (see his 'Wisdom', listed below). Although Knibb does not elaborate further on the specifics of his suggestion, it coheres well with the view that the author might be among the ranks of those learned Jewish leaders who, enlightened by their study of scripture, were seeking to formulate a Jewish way of life in a time when the temple was not functioning. 2 Baruch, in many ways the twin of 4 Ezra, gives strong indications of arising out of early rabbinic circles, and the same impression might be given by the text of 4 Ezra itself. So, towards the end of episode I (5.16-19), Ezra is met not by the people themselves but by Phaltiel, identified as 'a chief of the people'. Whatever the relationship between Ezra and Phaltiel, Ezra is acting in the service of the Jewish leadership who seek divine guidance on behalf of the people. If this literary feature has any correspondence with the historical situation of the author (such is not necessarily the case, of course), it might be that the author of 4 Ezra recognized himself to be within the ranks of those Yavnean Jewish leaders who were in the process of considering Jewish practice and piety in a post-destruction context.

If so, who was the author writing for? Perhaps he was writing to instruct a broad audience, but this view seems somewhat problematic. While 2 Baruch, with its confident assurance in God's faithfulness to Israel, advocates a theological stance that would be readily available for public consumption, the theological position presented in 4 Ezra seems much less amenable to this, because of the pessimism of the first three episodes and the description of salvation going to a number well less than the general population (on this, see especially Collins, Apocalyptic Imagination, pp. 177-80). So too, as we have seen, Knibb makes an intriguing suggestion that the book was written for the benefit of a group of learned men. In this regard, it is interesting to note that Ezra's relationship to the people changes throughout the text; if initially he is the people's spokesperson in a position of leadership (5.16-19), he later meets them again, still as a leader but now with eschatological mysteries that he cannot disclose to them (12.40-50; 14.1-48; again, there is little of this in 2 Baruch).

This issue, the public–private distinction of episodes V and VII, deserves fuller attention. Ezra is instructed to reveal the eschatological secrets only to the wise, not to the people. What is *not* said about these secrets needs to be noted. Other apocalyptic texts expect the divine revelations to be distributed throughout the general population (e.g. Jub. 1.4-7; 1 En. 82.1-3; 2 En. 33.8-11; 47.1-6) or to be kept hidden until the last generation when they will be disclosed to the public (e.g. 2 En. 35.2), but neither of these ideas is found in 4 Ezra, where it is clearly stated that those who are to know the secrets of God's eschatological ways are only the very few. That is to say, the author does not say that they should be distributed to the general public, nor does he make a temporal distinction between the time when Ezra received these private revelations and the time when they are to be revealed to the public. Instead, he simply makes a social distinction between those

who receive the seventy books and those who do not, without any
qualifications of any sort. The distinction in both episodes V and VII is
consistently a social rather than a temporal one, and Ezra is not
permitted to reveal the eschatological secrets of God to the corporate
people but only to the few who are wise. There is no suggestion that
the people are ever to gain access to the secret wisdom.

It might be argued that the public–private distinction is merely a
literary feature that cannot be used for purposes of social reconstruction. If this were the case, then this distinction would serve simply to
reinforce a sense of privilege among a wide readership who recognize
themselves to be included within the boundaries of the wise who are
conversant in the secret mysteries of God. Such a view, however,
seems difficult to square with the tone and dynamics of the text, and
reads 4 Ezra in the light of the literary strategies of other apocalyptic
texts rather than reading it for its own sake. Although we are in murky
terrain in considering whether the public–private distinction is a
literary feature or a social indicator, it appears more likely that it operates in the latter fashion, allowing us a glimpse into the social setting of
the text, which seems to have been written for a consciously distinct
group within the general population of Israel.

All these indicators seem to suggest that the author was a post-
destruction Jewish leader (probably a learned, pharisaic scribe) writing
exclusively for the benefit of a distinct group of Jewish leaders who
might have recognized something of themselves in the figures of Ezra
and Phaltiel. If this is the social setting out of which 4 Ezra arose, it still
remains to consider what the social function of 4 Ezra might have
been—that is, how the author hoped his text might operate within that
setting, how his learned audience were to be influenced, and in this
again the public–private distinction plays an important part, as will be
suggested below.

The Social Function of 4 Ezra

Some of the most important aspects of the author's project have already
been recognized and play a central part in his purposes: the high regard
for the law as the standard of salvation, the enormous eruption of
confidence in God in the later episodes, and the rethinking of traditional covenantal expectations. One further piece of evidence not yet
considered is also particularly relevant in this matter: that is, the
author's conservative tendency with reference to the hope for national

reconstitution by means of political insurrection against Rome.

Throughout the long narrative of 4 Ezra, a consistent pattern emerges that is indicative of the author's attitude on this matter. Uriel attempts in the first three episodes to undermine Ezra's interest in the reversal of Israel's fortunes in this world, and to turn Ezra's focus to the next world for the vindication of the righteous. That triumph comes about exclusively by means of divine initiative; never is there any indication that the righteous themselves lend assistance or play a part in the events whereby evil is overthrown and justice is established. The same is true of the visions in episodes V and VI, where the single focus is on the messiah. His activity is depicted in episode V in terms of a judicial court rather than a battlefield, and in episode VI he alone acts to overthrow evil 'without effort', his only instrument being the law (13.38). Moreover, the people who are gathered to him are not warriors in a holy conquest; they are a multitude who are 'peaceable' (13.12; interpreted as the exiled tribes, still identified as peaceable in 13.39, 47) along with a remnant whom he sets free (12.34) and defends while he (alone) destroys the multitude of the nations (13.49). No assistance is given by the remnant itself.

This is in marked contrast with some popular Jewish expectations of the day; the events of the first Jewish rebellion against Rome are themselves the clearest indication of this. So, too, in the Apocalypse of Abraham, a text contemporary with 4 Ezra, God speaks of the eschatological events as being 'an age of justice' (29.18) in which the righteous 'will destroy those who have destroyed them' and 'will rebuke those who have rebuked them through their mockery' and 'will spit in their faces' (29.19). The same sentiment is found even among members of the Qumran community who produced the Dead Sea Scrolls. Although their political quietism is notable, there is evidence of an eager expectation that the righteous community would aid the angels of God in the final eschatological battle between the Sons of Light and the Sons of Darkness (e.g. *The War Scroll*).

In 4 Ezra, however, there is nothing to encourage such a view; in fact, the narrative seems to foster an attitude of political quietism. Instead of nurturing an interest in overturning the people's present situation, the author wants to encourage quiet living among the people, whose sights should be set not on the reversal of their portion in the present age of evil but on the hope that they will be among those who are judged worthy to inherit the next world of marvel. The author seems intent on disabling any interest in organized measures devised to overthrow Rome and establish Israel's kingdom. Such expectations are rooted in an inadequate and misleading view of the covenant relationship between Israel and their God.

This is where the public–private distinction of episodes V (12.35-39) and VII (throughout) becomes grounded. The restriction of the eschatological ways of God to the circles of the wise is not indicative of some bland, idiosyncratic interest on the part of the author (e.g. the perpetuation of apocalyptic literature). Instead, it is his way of handling an urgent, pressing socio-political concern. (The very fact that it is highlighted throughout the final episode and is the point on which the book closes should signal its importance.) The author seems concerned to restrict eschatological interest to the arena of a select group of people who handle it appropriately without perpetuating the kind of social irresponsibility that results from fostering expectations concerning the overthrow of one's overlords. Matters concerning the end of this age when God will overthrow all other claimants to power and eradicate all evil—these matters are not to be the object of speculation within the ranks of the general population, but only among the wise. The people of Israel need only to be instructed in the ways of the law in an attitude of complete confidence in God. So, in Ezra's final speech to the people in 14.27-36, he offers them no assurance that God will restore the fortunes of the nation in this age; instead, all attention is focused on past misdemeanours and on the future day of judgement when all will be judged according to the standard of the law; the overthrow of Rome and of evil that was so graphically depicted in episodes V and VI is nowhere mentioned since these matters are not to be the concerns of the common people. Rather than instilling some expectation of or readiness for the reversal of the nation's position, the people are simply to concern themselves with living faithfully before God by keeping his law. With historical hindsight, the author's concerns in this matter were not persuasive enough to prevent another revolt from occurring within three decades (132-35 CE), under the leadership of Bar Kochba—a revolt that again ended in tragedy for the Jewish people.

In short, one of the author's pressing concerns is to establish a balance between social quietism and confidence in the God, whose justice ensures future retribution against Rome and all evil-doers. This confidence in God is to be encouraged as well as contained: encouraged, in that without it despair envelops all, motivation is dissipated, and faithfulness to the law is virtually impossible; contained, in that it needs careful supervision, to ensure that it does not deteriorate into a form of militant nationalism, rebellious revolt and active insurrection. Keeping the mysteries of God's eschatological activity from being promoted among the people is one measure in the careful management of the people's confidence in God.

4 Ezra, then, may be characterized as a book of definitions: grief and sorrow are defined as healthy characteristics of a post-destruction people only when they are kept within the context of certainty in the sovereignty of God, in distinction from the kind of despair that disheartens and paralyses; similarly, confidence and hope in God are defined as the healthy characteristics of a post-destruction people only when they are kept within the context of socio-political quietism, in distinction from a kind of irresponsible confidence, exuberance and fanaticism that results in aggressive uprising against one's oppressors.

In this way, one of the author's main purposes is to set out a double call: an explicit call to faithful living in accordance with the glorious law, and an implicit call to patience with regard to the political situation of the people. The righteous are those whose citizenship is with the heavenly city of brilliance, loveliness and splendour (10.50, 55), rather than with an earthly city. As people of the heavenly city, so they should seek earnestly to replicate the values of heavenly purity in their own lives, in accordance with the law of glory, in preparation for the heavenly treasures that await them. In the light of all this, any future restoration of the earthly city is somewhat irrelevant.

Summary of the Author's Project and Purpose

To summarize all that we have seen, it seems that the author of 4 Ezra was a well-established Jewish leader (most likely a learned scribe with Pharisaic sympathies), who wrote primarily (perhaps even exclusively) for the benefit of other Yavnean Jewish leaders involved in the enterprise of reconstructing Jewish belief, practice and piety in a post-destruction context. In his text (perhaps a kind of theological discussion paper, anachronistically speaking), he addressed the theological issues that perplexed him concerning God's covenant relationship with Israel, as he struggled to rediscover his confidence in God's sovereignty. This confidence was facilitated by the overpowering visions of the eschatological reclamation of the world by God through his messiah. These breathtaking visions inspired hope, and flooded the author's perception so fully that disturbing thoughts concerning Israel's prospects for salvation were overwhelmed by the awareness of the glorious prospects awaiting the righteous as a result of the extraordinary and unassisted efforts of the messiah. In the meantime, the author and his colleagues were to encourage a quietistic hope in God and to instruct all the people to keep the law of God; if obeying the law is a strenuous and daunting task, it thereby requires an overwhelming confidence in God as its prerequisite.

Further Reading

1. *On the social setting and social function of 4 Ezra*

M.A. Knibb, 'Apocalyptic and Wisdom in 4 Ezra', *JSJ* 13 (1982), pp. 56-74. Knibb proposes that 4 Ezra was written for a small group of learned men engaged in the study of Jewish scriptures and in interpretative writing.

P.F. Esler, 'The Social Function of 4 Ezra', *JSNT* 53 (1994), pp. 99-123. A thought-provoking article which employs several models of analysis (e.g. millenarianism, cognitive dissonance, introversionism, Russian literary formalism) in determining the social setting and function of 4 Ezra.

J.R. Mueller, 'A Prolegomenon to the Study of the Social Function of 4 Ezra', in K.H. Richards (ed.), *SBL Seminar Papers 1981* (Chico, CA: Scholars Press, 1982), pp. 259-68. Mueller tries to place 4 Ezra within post-destruction Judaism, seeing it as a work not of 'world maintenance' but of 'world reconstruction'. Mueller does nothing with the public–private distinction.

L.L. Grabbe, 'Chronography in 4 Ezra and 2 Baruch', in K.H Richards (ed.), *SBL Seminar Papers 1981*, pp. 49-63. Grabbe closes with a section considering whether 4 Ezra could have come from the hand of a post-destruction 'rabbi', and concludes that it might have.

M.E. Stone, 'The Question of the Messiah in 4 Ezra', in J. Neusner *et al.* (eds.), *Judaisms and Their Messiahs*, pp. 209-25, esp. 216-20. On the basis of the messianic portrait given in 4 Ezra, Stone wonders as to the kind of a social setting in which such a portrait would make sense.

M.E. Stone, 'On Reading an Apocalypse', in J.J. Collins & J.H. Charlesworth (eds.), *Mysteries and Revelations*, pp. 65-78, esp. 75-77. A more elaborate reconstruction than that given in 1987 (above), analysing relationship between literary characters as guides to social setting.

M.L. Gray, 'Towards the Reconstruction of 4 Esdras and the Establishment of its Contemporary Context' (BLitt thesis, University of Oxford, 1976). A discussion of basic issues and the theological perspective of 4 Ezra (especially 4 Ezra's views on knowledge and sin) leads Gray to conclude that the social setting is different from anything known to us from other Jewish sources of the time.

H.C. Kee, '"The Man" in Fourth Ezra: Growth of a Tradition', in K.H. Richards (ed.), *SBL Seminar Papers 1981*, pp. 199-208. In his analysis of episode VI, Kee postulates that 4 Ezra is written by a member of a small community of Jews who considered themselves to be the faithful remnant of Israel, while the leaders of the people (and the masses with them) had shown themselves to be unfaithful to God's ways.

J.A. Overman, *Matthew's Gospel and Formative Judaism: The Social World of the Matthean Community* (Minneapolis: Fortress Press, 1990), pp. 27-34. 4 Ezra emerges from a sectarian community convinced of its own faithfulness and of the unfaithfulness of the rest of the people, especially those in positions of power.

2. *General surveys of the social setting of Jewish apocalypses*

P.R. Davies, 'The Social World of Apocalyptic Writings', in R.E. Clements (ed.), *The World of Ancient Israel* (Cambridge: Cambridge University Press, 1989), pp. 251-71. A helpful article, examining useful definitions and recent research on the subject, and demonstrating the social origins of apocalyptic interest and the social setting of various apocalyptic texts.

G.W.E. Nickelsburg, 'Social Aspects of Palestinian Jewish Apocalypticism', in D. Hellholm (ed.), *Apocalypticism in the Mediterranean World and the Near East* (Tübingen: Mohr [Siebeck]), pp. 641-54. A review of past scholarship and a methodological investigation with a test case, recognizing the diversity of situation and function of various apocalyptic texts.

L.L. Grabbe, 'The Social Setting of Early Jewish Apocalypticism', *JSP* 4 (1989), pp. 27-47. A helpful study that shatters many traditional beliefs about apocalyptic literature rising out of disenfranchised, marginalized communities.

3. *On 4 Ezra as theodicy*

A.L. Thompson, *Responsibility for Evil in the Theodicy of IV Ezra* (Missoula: Scholars Press, 1977). Although often imposing its own agenda on the text of 4 Ezra, this detailed book offers helpful insight into the author's strategy and effectiveness as a theodicist (see especially his chapter 6).

T.W. Willett, *Eschatology in the Theodicies of 2 Baruch and 4 Ezra* (JSPSup 4; Sheffield: JSOT Press, 1989). Examines the role of eschatology in addressing theodicy-related issues; a somewhat unfocused and redundant study.

9

CHRISTIAN DEVELOPMENTS: 5 EZRA AND 6 EZRA

Christian Use of 4 Ezra

The text of 4 Ezra, like all Jewish apocalypses of Early Judaism, did not survive within Jewish circles, but was transmitted within the Christian church, where it played a part in nurturing the theological and liturgical life of various Christian communities. A few examples might suffice to show the extent of its influence.

The history of textual transmission itself demonstrates clearly the extent to which 4 Ezra circulated within early Christian circles. One textual critic has recently argued that the original Semitic text of 4 Ezra was translated into Greek, which itself spawned at least four other Greek versions (and no doubt more), each of which lies behind further translations into Latin, Syriac, Ethiopic, and Gregorian. This proliferation of the text into Greek translations at a very early stage, and later into various other languages, demonstrates the manner in which 4 Ezra was appreciated within the Christian church not long after its date of composition.

This is supported by the fact that church leaders of the patristic period knew of it and quoted it favourably. So, for instance, Clement of Alexandria (150-215) cites 4 Ezra 5.35 in Greek (*Stromata* 3.16). Cyprian (200-58) seems to allude to 4 Ezra 5.54-55 (*Treatise to Demetrianus*). Ambrose (340-97) cites 4 Ezra on at least seven different occasions (*de bono Mortis* 10, 11, 12; *de spiritu Sancto* 2.6; *de excessu Satyri* 1.2; *ad Horontianum*, Letter 34; *Commentarius in Lucam* 1.60).

4 Ezra has played a part in edifying early Christian piety and prayer. In 4 Ezra 8.20-36, Ezra gives a striking and heart-felt appeal to the eternal and faithful God to show mercy to his people. This section of

the apocalypse, known as the 'Confession of Ezra', shaped the liturgy of the worshipping church; the *Apostolic Constitutions*, a liturgical collection from the fourth century which comprises several established liturgical compositions, recites the second half of 4 Ezra 8.23 (*Apost. Const.* 8.7.6; cf. too 4 Ezra 7.103 with *Apost. Const.* 2.14), while the whole passage from 4 Ezra is cited in Latin liturgical manuscripts dating from between the eighth and fifteenth centuries.

The only unfavourable note in relation to 4 Ezra which remains among the literature of early Christian history is a comment made by Jerome. In his defence of prayers for the dead, Jerome argued against Vigilantius and others who found support for their rejection of prayers for the dead in 4 Ezra 7.105-115. Jerome writes defiantly against them: 'You bring before me an apocryphal book which, under the name of Esdras, is read by you and those of your ilk, and in this book it is written that after death no one dares pray for others. I have never read the book' (*Contra Vigilantium* 6). Despite Jerome's own ignorance of the text, his words reveal the way others Christians of his own day valued the Jewish apocalypse of 4 Ezra.

4 Ezra's influence is evident as well in a number of ancient Christian texts which seem to have been written in conscious dependence on 4 Ezra (or on a text which itself was dependent on 4 Ezra). In particular, these include four Christian apocalyptic texts: the *Greek Apocalypse of Ezra* (second to eighth century), the *Vision of Ezra* (fourth to seventh century), the *Questions of Ezra* (date uncertain), and the *Apocalypse of Sedrach* (second to fifth century). Each of these texts develop theological themes derived from 4 Ezra, amplifying them in a manner which suited their own theological inquiries.

Christian readers and scribes sometimes left their own fingerprints on the text of 4 Ezra. For instance, the reference in 7.29 to 'my son, the Messiah' was copied in the Latin manuscripts of 4 Ezra as 'my son, Jesus'. In 7.48, Ezra laments the condition of sin which permeates '*almost all* who have been created'. In some Christian manuscripts this was amended to speak of sin having infiltrated the lives of '*all* who have been created', thereby reinforcing rather than contradicting Paul's view in the New Testament of the universality of sin. So, too, it has been suggested that 4 Ezra 7.36-140, a section of the book which appears to have been 'lost' in the transmission of the text, is missing in almost all the extant manuscripts of 4 Ezra since it includes material which is problematic for the church's teaching about prayers for the dead and the possibility of second repentance after death (7.102-115; compare the debate between Jerome and Vigilantius, cited above). It may, then, not have been accidentally lost, but purposefully removed.

Finally, it is interesting to note that the shape of western history was influenced somewhat by 4 Ezra. In 6.42, Ezra speaks of God's creation being composed of seven parts, six of which are dry ground while the seventh is watery. Although this is not of course the case, Christopher Columbus quoted this verse as part of his appeal for financial assistance from the Spanish sovereigns in order to embark on a westward rather than eastward voyage to India—a successful appeal which resulted in his discovery of the 'New World'.

Lacking so far from this brief overview of the Christian use of 4 Ezra is any mention of the Christian texts 5 Ezra and 6 Ezra. These Christian works now appear before and after 4 Ezra in the larger text usually referred to as 2 Esdras, comprising 2 Esdras 1–2 and 2 Esdras 15–16 respectively. Since 6 Ezra is the more straightforward of the two texts, we will examine it first, leaving the intriguing issue of the historical and theological importance of 5 Ezra to the end.

6 Ezra: Encouragement to a Persecuted Christian Community

Although 6 Ezra (2 Esdras 15–16) survives only in the Latin text of 2 Esdras, it appears to have been written in Greek, perhaps as an appendix to a Greek translation of 4 Ezra, although it may originally been an independent text which was appended only later to 4 Ezra. It is likely to have been composed late in the third century CE, since some historical allusions are evident in the text. This is especially true of 15.28-33, which seems to allude in cryptic fashion to the invasions of the Persian army into Roman Syria in 259 CE under King Shapur I (240-73). By 260 CE, the Persian invasion looked secure (cf. 15.30), but this was only temporarily the case, and victory soon turned into defeat (cf. 15.31-32). Suggested allusions at other points in the text all correspond relatively closely to this dating of 6 Ezra late in the third century, and also help to locate the author somewhere within the eastern region of the Roman empire.

As it currently stands, 6 Ezra is linked to 4 Ezra in the first two verses. The command to 'proclaim to my people the words of prophecy which I give you to speak' (15.1) introduces no new character, and is intended to be addressed to the Ezra whom we see in 4 Ezra 14. Similarly, the command to write down the words of God (15.2) also links up with the instructions given to Ezra in 4 Ezra 14.

Although the content of 6 Ezra is not specifically Christian for the most part, it is nonetheless most likely to be a Christian document rather than a Jewish document that has been lightly revised with a few Christian touches. Its real import is not theological or doctrinal, but pragmatic, calling its addressees to persevere in the face of extreme persecution. So, the text begins by calling to mind the brutal experiences that the community faces: plots, oppression, violence, the spilling of innocent blood (15.3-9). This is the present context of the community in crisis, a community 'led like a flock to the slaughter' (15.10). So, too, the text ends by calling the community to endurance, for God will deliver those who do not fear persecution or doubt that God is in control as their guide (16.74-75). In the meantime, they are to obey God's commandments and keep sin at bay, for sinfulness will prove to be their undoing and will undermine their hopes for salvation (16.76-78). These themes were dominant in 4 Ezra, in relation to the Jewish community of the late first century CE; now they are being applied in the late third century CE for a community which may have known and treasured 4 Ezra.

Between the beginning and the end of the text, there appears an extended description of God's destruction of the enemies of his elect, as he takes control of his world and eradicates all those who stand in opposition to his way of righteousness. Here, in the spirit of recompense and vengeance, God proclaims: 'Just as they have done to my elect until this day, so I will do [to them]' (15.21; cf. 15.52-53). The increase in evil will serve the purposes of God, as evil rises up against evil and tears apart the fabric of society (e.g., 15.14-19, 46-63). God will initiate the destruction of sinners, delivering them over to 'death and slaughter' (15.26) by the sword, fire and calamity (15.22-23; 16.3-5, 21-34). Babylon and its power-network will be crushed by the all-powerful God.

Throughout the main body of the text, the author depicts a scenario of divine retribution upon the oppressors of the community in extreme terms so that community members will remain firm in their loyalty to God and to the community of his faithful people. To dissociate oneself from that community is to put oneself within the arena of those upon whom the divine persecution is soon to come. Faced with this option, community members will no doubt prefer the persecution of its oppressors to the persecution of the almighty and sovereign God who holds the power of the universe within his hands (e.g., 16.6-16, 55-62). His all-pervasive vision will spot any who seek to avoid their present sufferings by compromising their faithfulness to him, and their apostasy will be brought to light in judgement (16.51-67). Better it is to fear God's judgement (16.67) than to fear the threat of present persecution (16.75). God's triumph is soon to come (e.g., 16.35-39), and this knowledge should cause God's people to stand firm in their obedience to him (16.40-50).

In all this, then, 6 Ezra addresses a situation of persecution and places the anxiety of the community within the context of confidence in God as the one who has not abandoned them, and who will eradicate sin and oppression along with sinners and oppressors, to the benefit of those who remain faithful to him. The present situation of the anguished community is placed within the spectrum of God's eternal plan and control, and the addressees are encouraged to stand firm despite their distress. Persecution is not a sign of divine disfavour, as they might have thought, nor are the disordered currents of history indicative of a world out of control. Instead, all this is a part of the process of the beginning of the end, when all will be set right and God will reign supreme in communion with those who have obeyed him in full confidence and surrender throughout it all.

6 Ezra bears some obvious resemblances to 4 Ezra. Each is written at a time of crisis as an explanation of the way in which recent tragic events do not undermine faith in a sovereign and just God. Moreover, each looks to the eschatological triumph of God as the moment when all will be set right for those who are deserving, despite their present suffering.

5 Ezra: Christians claiming Israel's Privileges

5 Ezra is a text which (like 6 Ezra) has not attracted much scholarly attention. There is little consensus on some important matters in current scholarly study of 5 Ezra, and much work needs still to be done. Only a cursory investigation of possibilities can be given here, until such time as an informed scholarly consensus emerges.

The text of 5 Ezra survives in Latin primarily in nine manuscripts from the ninth to thirteenth centuries, eight of which include 4 Ezra and 6 Ezra, and all of which originated from mainland Europe, chiefly Spain and France. It was most likely written in either Greek or Latin, with the former being slightly the stronger of the two options. Nonetheless, even a Semitic original (Hebrew or Aramaic) cannot be ruled out, especially if (as some have argued) it was composed within Jewish rather than Christian circles.

It is possible that several stages of reworking and redaction lie behind the present form of the text. For some, this process originated with a Jewish author, whose work has been taken over into Christian circles and reworked with Christian emphases and content. For most, however, the work is by a Christian author who is deeply immersed in the Jewish scriptures and theological traditions, and this is the view adopted in this guide. The author's location is unknown (Egypt was advocated by one nineteenth-century scholar, but with few advocates; a more common suggestion is Rome, although this too has very poor evidence).

5 Ezra is normally dated somewhere between 130 and 250 CE. This is an important issue, especially if it was composed towards the earlier of these two dates, near the time of the Bar Kochba revolt in 132-35 CE in Judaea. G. Stanton and T.A. Bergren argue for precisely this early dating. Stanton, for instance, suggests that several considerations all converge on a date in the mid-second century, including the following points: (1) the apologetic strategy of 5 Ezra is typical of earlier Christian style, emphasizing the church's inheritance of Israel's privileges, whereas later Christian polemic is more oppositional, portraying Christianity and Judaism as two distinct and diametrically opposed entities (cf. the late second-century *Adversus Judaeos*, and Melito's 'Paschal Homily'); (2) 5 Ezra seems to be related to and prior to the late second-century text *Apocalypse of Peter*; (3) 5 Ezra's apocalyptic interests are more to do with the imminent end of time (e.g., 2.34, 41) than with the Anti-Christ and with elaborate portraits of heaven and hell, which are prominent marks of later Christian apocalypses (e.g., *Apocalypse of Peter*); (4) several passages in 5 Ezra depict a consciousness of the destruction of Jerusalem (135 CE) as a relatively recent phenomenon (e.g. 2.2-7), and are indicative of a conscious need to define the Christian church in relation to its Jewish parentage and contemporaries in ways which resemble earlier rather than later patterns. If these suggestions are correct, they support a mid-second century date for 5 Ezra, making it one of the few literary products of the Christianity of that time known to us.

The theological interests of 5 Ezra are relatively straight-forward. An extensive historical overview of God's dealings with Israel reveals the extent of his powerful acts of protection and benefit towards those whom he loves (1.9-23, 28-30a). Despite all this, however, Israel has sinned before God and has been unfaithful to his commandments (e.g.,

1.5, 6, 8, 24, 34; 2.1-5). This has resulted in Israel's being rejected by God (e.g., 1.25-27, 30b-34; 2.1-7), who has turned to others and given them his name (1.24; cf. 1.35-37; 2.10, 33-34). This group now keeps the law which Israel had not kept (1.24; 2.40) and thereby inherits the blessings which Israel has forfeited (2.10-12, expanded throughout 2.15-43)—most notably, resurrection from the dead and an eternal abode in heaven. If this group is distinct from the historical people of Israel (1.24, 35-36), it is also in continuity with Israel's divinely-ordained history (1.38-40), so that God can call them 'my people' (2.10), just as the term is used throughout the Jewish scriptures to identify Israel. This group who inherits Israel's name is vast (2.42), comprising those who are faithful to the Son of God (2.43 with 2.46-47).

In all this, lessons are being learned from Israel's history and applied to the Christian church. Retelling Israel's history reveals God to be merciful and loving, powerful and effective, towards those who obey him. His care extends past the earthly realm to the heavenly world, where a glorious and eternal reward awaits the faithful. The wonders of God's ancient dealings with Israel are far surpassed by the wonders of the future glory which he intended for Israel. And yet, Israel's sinfulness has disqualified them from God's promised blessings, which are now available to those who confess the name of the Son of God. In this way, Israel's history is the case-study from which lessons are drawn for the Christian audience of 5 Ezra, providing both a positive example of the rich blessings of God's love and a negative example of the dire consequences of human sinfulness.

The author himself is commonly thought to be a Jewish Christian. One does not read too far before discovering how thoroughly immersed he is in the texts of the Jewish scriptures. He maintains a high regard for the commands of God and is insistent that those whom God now calls 'my people' are also those who have kept God's law (1.14; 2.40). Moreover, he is concerned to show that God's rejection of Israel was not in God's original intention; in fact, God *pleaded* with Israel that he might be their God and father, and they his people and children (1.28-30).

Nonetheless, even if the author belongs to the race of the Jewish people, his ties are to the Christian community. Some commentators, in fact, think that he belonged to a persecuted Christian community. So, for instance, the 'dead' of 2.23-24 who are assured a heavenly rest may represent Christian martyrs, just as in 2.45-47 crowns are given to those who have laid aside the mortal body, perhaps symbolizing the final victory awarded to martyrs who have stood firm in the faith. 5 Ezra 1.26 may give further confirmation to this reading, depicting the Jews as those with blood on their hands. It is possible, then, that the persecution being alluded to was the Jewish persecution of Jewish Christians during the Bar Kochba revolt, when Jewish Christians were perceived as traitors to the Jewish cause. Nonetheless, it is not necessarily the case that these passages are indicative of persecution against Christians, or that there is a causal connection between them. If such a reading is granted, however, the destruction of the city of Jerusalem in 135 CE (cf. 2.4-6), which crushed the Bar Kochba revolt, would have been a significant event for our author, for whom allegiance to the Christian community took precedence and any ties to the Jewish community had dissipated. In fact, the destruction of Jerusalem had, in the mind of our author, resulted in the loss of any collective identity for the people of Israel, who had been 'scattered among the nations' and 'blotted out from the earth' (2.7)—notions which may be due more to the author's own psychological need for distance than to an empirical reality.

There are two further areas of theological and historical importance in 5 Ezra studies: first, the influence of the Matthean gospel within 5 Ezra and, second, the relationship between 4 Ezra and 5 Ezra. With regard to the first, Stanton has argued that the Christian author of 5 Ezra is steeped in the vocabulary and themes which rise to the fore in the Matthean gospel. This is especially true, he believes, of Matthew 21–25, where the canonical evangelist is particularly concerned with defining the relationship between the Christian church and the Jewish synagogue.

While Stanton may have exaggerated some of the details of his case, it is nonetheless evident that the Matthean evangelist and the Christian author of 5 Ezra share similar concerns, and that the latter has been influenced in large part by the former. While other New Testament influences can also be discerned within 5 Ezra, the Matthean influence is especially strong. Some of the more obvious cases where this is evident are: 5 Ezra 1.30 (cf. Mt. 23.37); 1.32 (cf. Mt. 23.37 and 18.34); 1.33 (cf. Mt. 23.38); 2.13 (cf. Mt. 7.7, 24.22, 25.34); 2.20-22 (cf. Mt. 25.31-46).

Most significant is 5 Ezra 1.24, which seems to be indebted to Mt. 21.43 (especially in view of the number of other parallels to Matthew 21–25). Both passages speak of God rejecting the Jewish people (or in the Matthean gospel, the Jewish leaders), as God's favour is transferred to another group—'a nation' that produces the fruit of the kingdom of God (Matthew), 'another nation' who will be given God's name and will keep his statutes (5 Ezra; the singular is generally preferred, rather than the plural 'other nations' that appears in the NRSV). This theme of rejection is concentrated in the Matthean gospel in the three parables which surround Mt. 21.43: the Two Sons (21.28-32), the Vineyard (21.33-41), and the Marriage Feast (22.1-14). It is a theme which the Christian author found to be particularly appropriate for building up the faith of his Christian community, who are assured of standing squarely in the caring sight of God, just as the people of Israel had done previously.

This kind of assurance would have been especially relevant in the aftermath of the Bar Kochba revolt. The misfortunes that befell the Jews as a consequence of that revolt were taken as evidence of the power of God against those who would be unfaithful to him. As such, Jewish misfortune became Christian encouragement, a point to which we will return below.

The second area of historical and theological importance is whether the Christian author of 5 Ezra knew the Jewish apocalypse of 4 Ezra. Although there is little scholarly discussion of this point, opinions are held on both sides of the matter. For some, 5 Ezra is an independent text, without any conscious development of the text of 4 Ezra, which may not even have been known to the author of 5 Ezra. In this scenario, the two texts became linked only at some later point. For others, however, 5 Ezra is most likely a Christian expansion of 4 Ezra, a Christian introduction to the Jewish apocalypse which clarifies, amplifies and redefines the theology of 4 Ezra, thereby acting as a prism through which 4 Ezra is to be read and providing an interpretative key whereby its contents are made relevant to a new and different audience.

If it can be shown that 4 Ezra was known by the author of 5 Ezra and provided the basis for his theological project, this might help to advance our knowledge of the relationship between Judaism and Christianity in the second century. Our Christian author's knowledge of 4 Ezra in the mid-second century may be one small indicator of a closer relationship between Judaism and Christianity in that period than is sometimes thought to have been the case. On the other hand, the same fact may not point to that conclusion at all, since others scenarios might be just as likely. For instance, if 5 Ezra and 4 Ezra can be shown to be genealogically related, this may be the result of some scribal storehouse of texts falling into the hands of Christian scribes after the Bar Kochba revolt, or having been accessible to both Jewish and Christian scribes (this is possible without much of an overlap in Judaism and Christianity, since scribalism was more of a professional occupation than a religious party or theology). All of this is quite speculative, and it may be that a clear solution will never emerge, but the possibilities are intriguing.

Apart from this historical issue, the possibility that 5 Ezra elaborates 4 Ezra raises some points of theological interest as well, since it allows us to see how an early Christian author might have read a Jewish theological text. The matter becomes more enthralling if 2 Baruch can also be shown to be a Jewish response to 4 Ezra. Three issues make for easy points of comparison.

First, 4 Ezra is pessimistic about the effectiveness of God's grace towards the ethnic people of Israel, since grace is (to all intents and purposes) absent from the present age. This same conviction is also evident in 5 Ezra, since God's favour, which is thought to be active within the present age, has nonetheless been transferred to 'another nation' beyond the boundaries of ethnic Israel. In 2 Baruch, however, the pessimism of 4 Ezra towards divine grace is overturned, and confidence in God's grace upon a repentant ethnic Israel is affirmed. If the author of 4 Ezra struggled to accept the kind of view perpetuated by the author of 2 Baruch, he shows not the least bit of interest in or cognisance of the kind of view articulated in 5 Ezra.

Secondly, 4 Ezra is extremely pessimistic about human ability to fulfil the law. While both 2 Baruch and 5 Ezra share a sense of the failure of Israel in this regard, neither of them despairs of the possibility of fulfilling the law *per se*. 2 Baruch is a clarion call for the people of Israel vigorously to obey the law, while 5 Ezra considers the law to be fulfilled by those within the Christian church. The author of 4 Ezra had difficulty believing that the former was possible for the majority of Israel, and gives no indication that the latter was even an option.

Thirdly, as a consequence of the first two points, 4 Ezra is pessimistic about the number who will enjoy God's salvation, identified as 'the few' (e.g. 8.3). This conviction has no currency within either 5 Ezra or 2 Baruch, where the number of those who will be saved is immeasurable—'a great multitude which could not be numbered' (5 Ezra 2.42), 'many, not a few, have proved themselves to be righteous' (2 Bar. 21.11).

It needs to be noted, however, that this kind of analysis springs from an assumption (still unproved) that the author of 5 Ezra (like 2 Baruch) was cognisant of 4 Ezra and elaborated the theological portrait given there. While this area of study might uncover new findings and prove to be fascinating in the long term, at present caution is advised, lest speculative hypotheses overstep the boundaries of acceptable reconstructions.

As a final word, it might be appropriate to comment on the techniques of self-definition evident within 5 Ezra, a text written to edify the faith of a Christian community whose members were to recognize themselves as God's chosen people and the recipients of his eschatological glory. The author, most likely a Jewish Christian, sought to strengthen their self-identity in relation to God, as a good pastor might be expected to do. But there may be a negative side to this, especially if 5 Ezra was written with the catastrophic events of 135 CE vividly in mind (as some have suggested). In that case, the author's attempt to edify his Christian audience is carried out by capitalizing on and exploiting the misfortunes of the Jewish people at one tragic point in their history—a technique which may have earlier precedent within some Christian texts but which may not be endearing to Christians today, in the wake of the holocaust against the Jews in the twentieth century. Perhaps the kind of polemic we see in 5 Ezra, which may have nurtured the faith of some second-century gentile Christians, should now be considered inappropriate—a relic of Christian history which needs perpetuating no further within Christian self-definition.

Further Reading

T.A. Bergren, *Fifth Ezra: Text, Origin and Early History* (Septuagint and Cognate Studies 25; Atlanta: Scholars Press, 1990). The only monograph on 5 Ezra, examining textual and historical issues.

T.A. Bergren, 'The "People Coming from the East" in 5 Ezra 1.38', *JBL* 108 (1989), pp. 675-83. Bergren examines how this phrase is rooted in a Jewish imagery that has been taken over into Christian polemic against Jews.

J. Daniélou, 'V Esdras', in his *Origins of Latin Christianity* (London: Darton, Longman & Todd, 1977), pp. 17-31. A helpful overview of the main theological themes of 5 Ezra.

G.N. Stanton, '5 Ezra and Matthean Christianity in the Second Century', *JTS* 28 (1977), pp. 67-83; reprinted in his *Gospel for a New People* (Edinburgh: T. & T. Clark, 1992), pp. 256-77. The influence of the Gospel of

Matthew upon the author of 5 Ezra is demonstrated and explored for its relevance within the author's social context.

R.A. Kraft, 'Towards Assessing the Latin Text of "5 Ezra": The "Christian" Connection', in G.W.E. Nickelsburg and G.W. MacRae (eds.), *Christians Among Jews and Gentiles* (FS K. Stendahl; Philadelphia: Fortress Press, 1986), pp. 158-69; also appeared in *HTR* 79 (1986), pp. 158-69. Argues that 5 Ezra is a Jewish document, later touched up by Christians.

J.H. Charlesworth, 'Christian and Jewish Self-Definition in Light of the Christian Additions to the Apocryphal Literature', in E.P. Sanders (ed.), *Jewish and Christian Self-Definition* (Philadelphia: Fortress Press, 1981), II, pp. 27-55. The themes of 5 Ezra and 6 Ezra are discussed in relation to those of 4 Ezra (pp. 46-48), as examples of Christian expansions of Jewish texts.

P. Geoltrain, 'Remarques sur la diversité des pratiques discursives apocryphes: l'exemple de *5 Esdras*', *Apocrypha* 2 (1991), pp. 17-30. An analysis of Christian use of Jewish apocalyptic texts, looking in particular at the way in which theological themes in 4 Ezra are developed in the mid-second century CE by the Christian author of 5 Ezra.

INDEXES

INDEX OF REFERENCES

OLD TESTAMENT

INDEX OF AUTHORS